David M. Lubeski – 1974

There are four seasons and four basic directions on the compass. There are also four primary directions of the wind. And I have been told that there are four points to the universe....this is my personal journey with them all.

Preface

The lobsters are pretty much gone now. And with them the boats and fleets and fishermen that pursued them. In the natural order of our world when one species goes into a decline another or others take over.

Lately, in speaking with some of my former fellow fishermen, there won't be a viable lobstering industry in the sound for at least the rest of our generation. They've begun the 'V' notch program to protect mature egg bearing females; however the short term outlook still looks quite bleak.

The book wasn't written to be a historical account of lobstering in Long Island Sound, but I feel that this aspect of the book might enlighten people in regards to its fragile existence.

I'm happily aware of the new generation's focus on the Body, Mind, and Spirit and a healthy lifestyle. Much of my book tries to emphasize the fact that there's one more aspect that's fundamentally important to achieve the inner circle of wholeness and well being, and that is our connection with Mother Nature.

There are four seasons, and four basic directions on the compass. There are also four primary directions of the wind. And I have been told that there are four points to the universe. Being a fisherman and hunter for over 35 years has given me a deep sense of connection and respect for our natural environment. And I've seen this time and time again in regards to my fellow fisherman and hunters.

Throughout the entirety of my book, one may appreciate the changes of the seasons on the water, the common bond of fishermen and nature, and just some good old fishing stories.

The book also focuses on maintaining a simple lifestyle, and the awareness of exploitation and the importance of conservation.

Lastly, however, perhaps most importantly, there's an emphasis in regards to being a good helper, paying attention to your natural environment, and handing down old traditions and means of survival. If it weren't for the old timers coaching me along and encouraging me throughout my lengthy fishing career, this book would have never been written. And I feel that I was chosen to hand their stories, along with mine, down.

Table of Contents

Chapter 1
Old Clown Shoes

The aluminum screen door emitted a long loud creak in the early morning stillness. Joe was sitting in his usual spot, behind the counter with the glass shelves and heavy glass top that displayed all the new fishing reels for sale.

Davey never looked at Joe first. To the right was a large stainless steel and glass icebox, which more often than not had Joe's morning catch, or part of it, displayed over a generous bed of crushed ice.

Davey would radiate to the front of the cooler, grasp his fingers behind the thin stainless steel top frame, and gaze in awe at the strikingly beautiful big blues or stripers. They were always so perfectly preserved he'd often wonder if they were still alive and just asleep.

A simple framework of braided nylon rope strung through thin metal rods, hung from the low ceiling. Joe's custom made fishing rods were spread out on top of the homemade net, along with a few popular commercially made types.

Along the wall behind the counter and long ice case, was a colorful array of fishing lures and hooks and leaders of a seemingly endless variety. The other walls had specialized equipment displayed from floor to ceiling. Minnow traps, crabs nets, all kinds of boots, clam rakes and landing nets of all shapes and sizes. Joe's little bait and tackle store had just about anything one needed in regards to any type of water related recreational activity, along with some commercial fishing supplies as well.

After a long wonderstruck look at the fish, Davey turned to Joe. His dark brown eyes, with just a little ring of dark blue around the pupil, seemed to be looking right through Davey, into some far off place. One couldn't see much of his face. Most of it was hidden behind an intensely curly, salt and pepper beard that sprung wildly from just below his eyes in seemingly every direction. His long, wild hair matched the beard, only growing from the opposite end of his head, and was even longer.

What you could see of his face was a dark, leather like tan on his cheeks, nose, and forehead. His weather-beaten face was fairly well wrinkled and scarred. His sizable nose extended first out and then down, curling back up just below his upper lip.

He almost always could be seen wearing a heavy long-sleeved plaid cotton shirt and tattered blue jeans. In the summer it was the same attire, only with stringy cutoff jeans and the sleeves rolled up on the shirt.

"Going down to see the clown shoes Davey?" Joe smiled at the boy and with that the wrinkles massed together under his eyes, the whole mass of flesh curled up like a quarter moon, and his eyes themselves began to water and shine.

"What do you mean Joe is there a circus down at the town dock?" Davey asked in reply.

"Well you might say that," Joe answered, smiling down at the twelve year old lad with the long, thick sun bleached wavy hair. "Just don't get too close. Go sit with the old timers on the rocks behind the 'Legion'. Watch everything from up there. You're higher up on the rocks and you could see the whole bay. It's a nice, bright quiet morning, so make sure that you look all around you. Don't forget to stop in on your way home; I wanna know how the fishing is."

"O.K. Joe," the boy replied, "by the way nice fish." Davey's feet were out the door but his head was turned for one last look at the oversized fish shining in the cooler.

Davey never asked Joe where he caught the fish. Joe had a boat and fished mostly early in the morning and came home shortly after sun-up. Davey loved to fish and loved to learn things about the ocean and fishing. He had his snapper blue rod, his bait, his pail, and most importantly in the twelfth summer of his life, he had a new blue Schwinn bike with a white banana seat with high handle bars and a wheely bar. He had transportation. He could go to the Point every morning.

Davey scurried excitedly out of the store, grabbed his gear and pedaled the quarter mile down the road. First he went along the high stone wall that separated the road from the grassy park with the tall row of "big swings". Then he was down onto the sidewalk with its chrome-painted, round steel rail that separated the road from the town beach. Then he pedaled down past the "American Legion Hall" and the high rocky outcropping that projected out into the bay behind the white building with the open front porch and salt grass green roof. Then he went past the low stone wall that dropped off in a pile of giant granite rubble connecting "little beach" at the town dock.

After weaving through an unusually large number of cars and trucks parked every which way in what was usually a small organized assembly of vehicles, Davey was suddenly staring at a very unusual experience.

Normally there were a handful of peaceful fishermen sitting at the edge of the dock. Some held their rods in their hands while others set them in the long, white plastic rod holding tubes that were nailed into the pilings spaced about six feet apart and running the entire two hundred feet of the old heavy wooden planked dock.

Men lined the dock from one end to the other, shoulder to shoulder casting and reeling at a high rate of speed, every type of artificial lure one could imagine. Poles arched and pulsated against the power of hooked fish. People were frantically casting, reeling and shouting. A large flock of seagulls, a few hundred feet out in the middle of the mouth of the river, were crying, flying and diving into the water, adding to the confusion. Fish were being hauled, flapping in mid-air in great numbers onto the dock. These large, glistening bluefish also seemed to have a wild, frenzied look in their eyes as they were being lurched from the water and hit the heavy wooden planks with a loud "smack". They were so full of energy that their bodies flailed wildly and their powerful jaws snapped helplessly at the plastic or metal "fish" with all those sharp hooks that was the means of their demise.

Davey looked over towards the rocks behind the Legion, walked his bike over and leaned it against the porch railing. Then he carefully negotiated the natural stone staircase which led to the highest point of the granite outcropping on the Eastern side of the harbor that had been smoothed out by millions of years of exposure to the sea, and sloped gradually down to the water's edge.

Three fishermen sat on upturned five gallon plastic pails, rods in hands, their eyes looking out into the vast distance of the sound. To their left, each of them had another pail with a wooden cutting board on top. Their fresh baitfish and bait knife glistened brightly in the morning sunshine. That pail also held their other basic gear. This included pliers, extra hooks and wire leaders, sinkers and a couple of dry rags stowed neatly inside. Nothing fancy, just enough to keep it a stress-free simple event.

Davey kept his distance. He knew that this big blue fishing was serious business. He knew the three fishermen, and he knew that they didn't want to be bothered right now.

Davey thought back to what Joe had said to him just a short while ago. Go up on the rocks, it's a nice bright calm clear morning. Go sit with the old timers and be sure to look all around you.

So the boy found a flat spot on the granite rocks, with the

waves of time furrowed in layers, much like the parabolic ridges and gullies of an exposed sandbar, and sat down.

It truly was a splendid morning. The day was becoming brighter as the sun climbed higher above the town dock, warming Davey's back and illuminating the whole scene in a surrealistic glow.

Davey looked out toward the open sound and then to his left and right. He perceived that the harbor was cradled by two long, high bright granite arms. It was almost like his outstretched arms holding a large ball or basket, so large that his fingers were about a foot away from each other to complete the circle, that's where the sound came in.

In the middle of the space between the two arms of stone lie two small islands known as the "Mermaids." The western rock is larger and more prominent than its sister to the east. Perched atop the western Mermaid is what looks like a large chrome and green box. At nighttime it's flashing light beckons through the narrow channel that runs between her and her little sister.

Beyond the two curling, sheltering arms, beyond the tireless flashing light atop the rigid white rock, lies the untamed world of the open sound.

The eastern arm of the harbor is a high granite bluff thickly tangled with scraggly old pines; its high smooth stoned hand cups the harbor's waters at about the same distance from the head of the harbor to the reach to the Mermaids. It then curls for a ways and parallels the river's course back towards the mouth. This arm terminates into a small rocky point, surrounded by a sand spit known as First Point. This little point forms the southern mouth of the river. The outer tip of this arm is known as Second Point, which forms the mouth of that side of the harbor.

The western arm of the harbor is much longer and holds several small beaches. The landscape is much more open and the shoreline is lined with colorful summer cottages.

To the west of the rocks behind the "Legion" lies the town beach which also includes a sloping grassy park. The beach curves inland from the edge of the rocks, runs straight for three hundred yards or so then curves back out towards the sea. The shoreline then becomes rocky again and rises up into another high stone ledge that juts out, then around into another little hidden bay. Then there's another high rock wall, hidden by the first then another muddy beach then another arm forms and curves out to the sea. So there's three bays within the bay, each one different but part of the whole.

Davey looked down toward the dock. People were walking away from the edge with fish in both hands. Other people were milling around their cars and trucks while others kept fishing. The seagulls seemed much less frenzied, flying upriver a ways then turning back and flying out past the dock a ways out into the harbor, heads turning, constantly studying the surface of the water. Suddenly they regrouped in a tight pack just above the water, their wings fluttering rapidly for a moment before they dove quickly beneath the surface and re-appeared with wings flapping wildly on the surface.

Davey studied their pattern, which took them in a big circle just a short distance from shore around the entire bay. After awhile the flock was passing just off the shore of the town beach and heading towards the rocks where Davey and the three fishermen patiently sat, then the birds were directly out in front of them, not a hundred feet from the edge of the rocks.

Whitey stood up, rod in hand, never saying a word, never turning his head, just looking out to sea. Then he bent low towards the water, pointed his rod down to the horizon, waited what seemed to be a predetermined few seconds, then pulled back and up with a powerful, purposeful thrust. "Fish on" he yelled in a deep confident voice. His two comrades groaned to a standing position, and with backs hunched from age and time, reeled in their baits and set their rods down on the rocks.

Davey and the two old timers intently watched the struggle. Whitey methodically lowered and pumped back on the violently wrenching rod. And with that he would lower the end of the rod towards the edge of the rocks, and with sudden bursts of unbelievable energy, the fish would pull line off of Whitey's reel, and he could only hang on and wait for the energy to subside. The battle went back and forth in this manner for several minutes, and then Whitey made his move.

Whitey was a tall, strikingly handsome man, with a square, rocklike jaw and hair the color of new snow which shined so brightly in the strong morning sunlight. He nimbly began maneuvering down the steep rocky slope, never looking down, never taking his eye off of the spot where his line entered the water. It was amazing to Dave y how sure-footedly and fluidly an old man with a busted up body and a wooden leg (his real one was blasted off in the war) could negotiate that difficult terrain. At the water's edge were several fairly large, flat seaweed covered rocks. It was standard procedure to make one's way down and onto one of these spots in an attempt to hand haul his quarry ashore.

The old man eased his way into position. The line was now close at hand where it entered the water. In one quick motion he let go one hand from its clutch on the rod, reached down into the water, grabbed the steel leader and hauled the long, flapping silver creature from the sea.

After that he proceeded to scurry up the rocks, limping heavily, dragging his fish behind. The old man sat on his pail and admired his catch. Both fish and fisherman were exhausted from the battle. They looked into each other's eyes, the fish occasionally flapping and gasping for air. With a series of slow, deep breaths, Whitey slowly regained a normal breathing pattern.

He then proceeded to remove the wooden cutting board from the adjacent bucket, and produced a long, clean, bright knife. Carefully he filleted the meat from both sides of the still twitching bluefish. Then he placed the fillets in a plastic bag and put it in the shade of the bucket. After cleaning the blood from the knife and his hands, he rose up, grabbed the carcass, and flung it back into the sea.

"The crabs gotta eat too," he said softly to himself.

Those were the only words spoken on that bright, clear morning on the 'fishing rocks", behind the "Legion", overlooking the sound.

Davey took one long last look around the harbor and out into the open sound. He then got up and walked down the natural stone staircase and on over to the town dock.

The crowd had disappeared, save for a handful of fishermen aimlessly casting and retrieving their lures into the mouth of the river. But as Davey approached, he noticed that the fishermen weren't the only creatures on the dock. Scattered about were several dozen large bluefish. They looked dull and dry in the warm morning light. They had dried out so much that their tails had curled up considerably, and arched from the heavy, wooden bloodstained planks.

Then Davey remembered his talk with Joe. It had been only a few hours earlier but now seemed like a long time ago. He looked down at the fish, all dried out and curled up, like a pile of old clown shoes.

Davey stood for a moment on the dock, and looked all around one last time. He looked up the river, then out and around then over to the "fishing rocks". He decided not to do any fishing that morning as the best hour for fishing, the first hour of light, had long since passed. Instead he slowly walked back to his bike, gathered his gear and began the trip home.

He didn't stop at Joe's. So much had happened that morning. So much was still fresh in his mind. He pedaled down the long straightaway, trying to put it all together. It seemed as if he was recalling a dream, a clear and vivid dream. But he knew it was all real and that he surely was a part of the whole experience.

Chapter 2

Snapper Blues

Albie sat alone at the end of the dock, patiently cutting up small pieces of fish and flipping them out into the river. A massive swarm of gulls hovered overhead, frantically screaming, diving and fighting over the fresh treats.

He'd already finished fishing for the day, his long bamboo rod laid alongside a pail which was covered by a soaking wet rag. The pail contained just enough fish for his own supper and the army of stray cats that made their home amongst the stacks of wooden lobster traps and myriad of other commercial fishing gear scattered about his backyard.

Albie was a reclusive man, he was usually out in his boat, but occasionally he would go down to the dock during snapper season, always early in the morning before anyone else arrived, to "shake the dust" as he would put it, off of his ancient bamboo pole, and feed the gulls.

Maybe the loss of his older brother, caught in a sudden storm out in the sound, was the reason for his reclusive, quiet nature. Maybe it was because he never got married and had a family of his own. Maybe it was some experience he had in the war. Whatever the case may have been, Albie and Davey were friends.

The boy edged up alongside Albie. The old man with the long dark brown face looked over and smiled at the boy, displaying five or six long dark brown teeth.

Albie knew Davey's family. They had lived in the same neighborhood for generations, as with most people, Dave's meetings with the "Polish Prince" were occasional to say the least, up to this point in his life anyhow, and this occurrence was no exception.

"You're Stanley's boy, aren't you?" He always greeted Davey in this manner, seemingly reassuring himself that his memory was still fully intact. Davey only nodded, keeping his eyes focused on the feeding swarm of gulls. "Good man Stanley, any man is a good man that could work in the Mill and raise five kids."

For a long time after that, there were no words spoken between the two friends. The early morning silence was broken only by the varied cries and clucking of the gulls. The old man seemed to delight in sharing his catch with everything around him. He'd cut up a handful of small chunks of fish and gently draw them close to his side in his massive grotesquely twisted hand. He'd throw most of the pieces out into the river and when the seagulls reacted, he would quickly slip the balance straight down into the water between the pilings.

"Crabs gotta eat too," he muttered, as if talking to himself. He then carefully cut a whole fish into very small pieces. He began throwing them into the swirling current of the river one at a time. "Now they'll teach the young ones how to survive," he said to the boy.

Davey studied the scene unfolding in front of him. The flock of seagulls was no longer flying in a confused manner overhead. It had let down onto the surface of the river in a tight group, right in front of the old man and the boy. Their orange webbed feet paddled rhythmically in an effort to maintain their position.

"How can you tell the young ones from the old ones?" Davey asked. It was late summer, and the young birds had shed their mottled white and brown plumage. Save for individual markings, they all looked about the same.

"Just listen to them talk," Albie replied. For a few minutes he refrained from feeding the birds. They began clucking, whistling and crying, impatiently, trying to coax their friend into continuing the feast.

"Look for the ones that make a high pitched 'wheee;'" Albie let out a series of whistles. First like the one that he wanted his friend to focus on, then he continued on with an array of different sounds, almost as if he were communicating with the creatures.

He waited a bit, and then asked the boy, "You see the young ones now?"

"Yeah, I hear the difference," Davey replied. "That high piercing whistle almost sounds like a baby crying."

"Mark it well," the old man said. He always used that saying when he wanted the boy to pay his fullest attention.

He began flipping one piece of fish at a time out to the birds, which had formed a tight circle on the surface of the river, right in front of the two spectators. It seemed to the boy that this wasn't the first time that this event had taken place. It seemed as if it had happened many times before, and now after so many rehearsals, the show was about to unfold.

One of the younger birds would make a quick attempt for a tasty morsel as it landed in the middle of the circle. It would be brutally attacked and driven off by one or more of its elders. Some of the yearlings would retreat to the outside of the circle and just mill around anxiously. Others would persist, moving quickly away, but staying close to the center following their harsh rebuttal. Time and time again, this handful of youngsters would attempt to win the offering. The older birds were relentless in their tormenting of their young.

Then after awhile the older birds would feign an attack when the food was tossed, and let the yearling retrieve, and immediately consume its reward.

"What'll happen to the ones that flew to the back of the circle?" the boy asked. "They didn't get anything to eat."

"They'll be alright lad," the old man softly replied. "Just take a good look all around you. Seagulls are a lot like people. Lots of them enjoy being in the company of others, like the flock out here in front of us. But take a good look around the bay and you'll see lots of birds that just like to be alone. Nature will provide plenty for them to survive on. The ones that went to the outside of the circle have made their choice. They'll be the ones that go their own way and learn on their own, but if you watch them close enough, you'll see that these loners will still keep in touch with the main flocks."

"You'll see that the individual birds are the ones that cry out the loudest, fly the swiftest and have the most confidence in themselves."

"Mark it well boy," the old man said as he slowly turned to look the pensive lad straight in the eyes. "You'll gain knowledge from going to school, reading books, and listening to other people's thoughts and ideas throughout your lifetime. But you'll gain wisdom from your own experiences, if you take the time and let their meaning come to you."

Albie then turned his head and stared squinting, out beyond the harbor walls, onto the sparkling brilliance of morning sunlight reflecting off the open vastness of water. He took a series of long deep breaths his eyes now nearly completely shut, his lips quivered gently, almost as if he were talking to someone that Davey couldn't see.

Then he put his head down and looked closely into the swirling waters below. His fingers groped along the wooden planks of the pier until he finally grasped the familiar hard roundness of his bamboo rod. As he stood up, rod in hand, and reached down for his pail he again looked deeply into Davey's eyes. "Gettin crowded, time to go." Mark it well lad, mark it well. See you on another tide."

With that, Albie was gone and Davey was alone with his thoughts. Davey wished that Albie would come around more often. It seemed like they had been friends for a long time and that they just became fuller of life after each meeting that they shared together.

Davey gazed out onto the river, which sparkled like millions of multicolored fish scales in the new morning sun. Then he looked around and saw that the whole length of the dock was filled with fishermen. It seemed like when he was looking out onto the water still thinking about the time he had just spent with his friend, that he was in one world and that when he looked up and realized everything that was happening around him, it felt that he was waking up in a different world. The snapper blues were in heavy and the circle went on.

Snapper blue season is a time for young fishermen to begin their careers and old fishermen to continue their ambitions. When these immature bluefish invade the coastal waters of the sound, ranging in length from six to ten inches, they can be caught with light spinning gear using lures, flies, or fresh bait. Most of the old timers however, preferred to apply the simplicity of a long, knobby often one piece bamboo rod with no reel. Attached to the single round metal tip which was usually fastened to the end of the pole with dull red single strand nylon thread was a short length of monofilament line, never longer than the rod itself. Three of four feet from the end of the line there was a float attached, sometimes it was a red and white plastic float, but more often than not it was some homemade painted wooden device that took on a variety of shapes and colors. Below the float was a small pinch of weight to keep the bait down in the current.

The old timers seemed to have an unspoken ritual during snapper season. They would arrive at the dock before sunrise and take up their customary positions, sitting down between the pilings and gazing out into the predawn light. Then they waited for Snowshoe.

Snowshoe was the bait man. He had a long, hand drawn seine net with a pole attached to each end. While the fishermen waited, Snowshoe, a cheerful old gent who always wore white cutoff shorts and nothing else regardless of the weather, and a previously agreed upon helper would take the net down to water's edge of the adjacent town beach.

Snowshoe would produce a can of sardines from his back pocket. After peeling away the cover, he would patiently knead each individual fish into a pungent, creamy mass and toss it a short distance into the water. After waiting a few minutes, and it seemed to be exactly the same amount of time, "Shoe" would slowly walk the net out until he was neck deep in the water. His helper would remain on shore, keeping the net upright and tight. Then "Shoe" would make a slow half circle back towards shore. He would rhythmically cup his free hand and splash a plume of water towards the outside edge of the net in an attempt to spook his quarry towards shore.

It was always amazing to Davey to see Snowshoe's net come ashore. The belly of his net was always so vibrant and colorful and full of life.

After the net had been dragged a safe distance from water's edge it was laid open. Snowshoe would personally cull out the largest shiners into his own pail. The remainder of the fish were drawn into a tight mass in the middle of the net and dumped into other pails. Snowshoe's helper would then bring the fresh supply of bait over to the dock and pass it out to the waiting fishermen.

Snowshoe's fresh bait was the best. The snapper blues fought themselves for it. And in the frenzy, the old fishermen seemingly recovered the agility and energy of their youths. Davey took great enjoyment in observing this event, old men becoming kids again. And Davey fished too, and he caught his fair share. Just enough for supper his mom would say to him, and a few for the cats.

It didn't take long to get enough. Soon the "out of towners" would be filtering in, looking for a spot to fish. One by one the early morning crowd gave up his spot for someone else, and went home feeling richer from the experience. So that was "snapper fishing" in the morning. Davey shared the sunrise, excitement and simplicity of the fishery, and brought home a nice fresh, tasty supper.

Evenings at the Point were totally different from the mornings in snapper season. The area immediately adjacent to the dock was packed with cars and the dock was packed with people fishing and people watching people fish. Small groups of people gathered amongst themselves, talking and laughing and just enjoying the cool breeze and peaceful environment.

Knowing the river's waters would share its predictable bounty of unseen life, knowing that its waters would enrich the awaiting brown sodden banks and beaconing green marsh grass, gently bending and drawing the rising waters ever so gradually into itself on a light cool evening breeze and awaiting that reunion and exchange of life the bait fish were always there. And the snappers knew that this is the way it always has been and always will be. And they swam by the thousands upriver with the incoming tide, scattering the schools of bait fish, getting nourishment and creating nourishment for other forms of life. So being at the mouth of the river the town dock and adjacent flat rocky point was the most productive place to fish. The summer folks and out of towners piled in every evening. Branford's native fishermen, over the years, had come to accept the desire of unfamiliar people to be part of their unbroken, traditional cycle. Instead of fighting for a spot on the dock or the rocks alongside, which would have surely guaranteed a fine catch, the natives chose to fish the quiet openness along the rocks behind the Legion, and the town beach below.

Davey liked to fish the beach in the evening. It was fun for him to kick off his shoes and wade out knee deep in the cool clear water. He enjoyed being at sea level, casting his shiny silver lure out into the mysterious darkening ocean. Everyone fished with lures from the beach. The fish were scattered and more water could be covered by casting one's lure to a different spot each time. When a fish was taken, the next cast would be directed in the same location in hopes that there was a small school of feeding snappers working that particular spot. The same group of people assembled on the beach every evening and fished, not talking much, but just soaking up that brief, intimate, beautifully simple and peaceful time of year.

After the Labor Day weekend, lots of things would change. Up until then, Davey had spent every day weather permitting, enjoying his summer down at the point. He'd wake up each morning full of excitement, quickly dress, grab his fishing rod and pail, hop on his awesome new bike and navigate in the predawn light the one mile route which almost seemed to have become a part of him, down to the town dock. He'd fish with the old timers at sunup. Then when the dock was passed on to the quickly growing crowd, he would descend onto the rocks alongside the dock at the mouth of the river, and clean his catch.

First he'd snap off their heads with his thumbs and forefinger and throw them into the river. Then he'd reach up into the body, pull out the guts, and flip them onto the rocks. A quick rinse in the river and they were cleaned and into the pail. That was that. Quick and easy. Pure and simple.

After he climbed up off of the rocks and back onto the dock, he'd look back. Seagulls had overtaken the spot where he had been cleaning the fish and were feeding on the tender fresh treats that Davey had left for them. And he knew, but could only imagine in what way, that the heads at the bottom of the river were nourishing some other creatures too. That gave Davey a sense of contentment as he slowly pedaled home.

Davey went back home mainly to get his fresh catch safely in the refrigerator. He'd take everything out of the sink, run the cold water and dump in the fish. During the final rinse, he reflected on the morning's trip. Each time, he thought, he did many things in the same manner; however each trip brought something different and unique. Maybe it was an unusually spectacular sunrise, or someone pulling up a rare species of fish or some earthly or unearthly cloud pattern that he had watched from its conception to maturity then dissolve in the bright morning sky. Maybe it was the way dawn's light brought warmth and color to the earth and sparkled like a million shimmering diamonds on the water in the morning's first breeze. Whatever the reason, perhaps it was all of these and more, in Davey's mind he longed to be back at the Point. So he'd wash up, have a bite to eat, pester his mom for a "couple bucks", grab a beach towel and be on his way.

Although Davey enjoyed fishing the most, there was a lot more for a twelve year old boy to do at the Point during his summer vacation. After leaving his bike in the long metal rack inside the two massive stone pillars at the entrance to the park and getting a long drink from the trusty water fountain, he'd usually go down to the beach. He liked to lie down on the warm sand and think and just relax. The strong summer sun warmed him to his innermost parts and he would stare at the infinite individual grains of sand, listening to the gentle unbroken song of the waves, feeling the cool caress of the light steady breeze which brought the smells of foam and seaweed heavy and pungent in the moist air. Davey felt distant from everyone else around him yet part of the soothing sand below his body, the waves kissing the shore and the sweet smelling breeze in the sky. As he breathed, the whole earth seemed to be taking long, deep relaxing breaths hoping to hold onto the season forever. After taking in some sun and a little quiet time by himself, Davey would look around for some company. In the summers of his youth, at the town beach there weren't many people that he didn't know. Usually there'd be a handful of his schoolmates that got together and mostly they went swimming. There are lots of places to swim at the Point, some in the river and many in the bay. Each spot offered the same basic elements of getting cooled off and refreshed and getting a good heart pumping workout. However each one was totally physically different from the other in its natural characteristics and held the power to bring forth different emotional experiences. Instinctively, even in their youths, the group knew the right time to enjoy each unique location to their fullest advantage.

The dock area presented two special swimming activities, from mid-tide on up to the flood and then back down again till the middle of the out-going. It was the perfect time to jump or dive off of the upstream end of the dock. There's a fairly high stone seawall atop of which is fastened a round silver metal railing that runs at right angles towards the end of the dock forming one side of the parking lot. About fifty feet from where the planks of the dock meet the wall, there's a metal gangplank which leads down to a large square floating pier held in position by a towering wooden piling in each corner. The floating pier, the seawall and the dock provided a perfect manmade half circle of fun and excitement for the gang.

They dove and jumped, and splashed each other. And they dunked heads. And they got to know each other, physically and mentally in a very basic but intimate manner. There were also personal challenges presented to the youths at each swimming spot. At the dock, one thing to consider was to climb up on top of the corner piling, gather one's balance and composure and dive off into the air, with the water's surface being anywhere between fifteen to eighteen feet below, depending on the tide. It seemed safer to just jump for many of the youths. Maybe it was because one could pull themselves quickly back to the surface, whereas when a dive was performed, the person was subject to the mysterious and unknown depths of the river. Davey liked to dive off of the piling.

Another exciting event was to hold onto the side of the float and take a deep breath of air, then throw one's self underwater and swim underneath the float, popping up into one of the air chambers created between the hulking barnacle covered styrofoam forms, which provided buoyancy for the floating wooden dock above.

Davey's favorite and most challenging experience in that environment was swimming across the river. Two hundred yards of strong, dark swirling current separated the dock from the opposite sandy shore lined with year round houses. Swimming across the river called for very careful timing. White diving and floating around with his friends, Davey always kept an eye on the rows of bleached white pilings that lined both sides of the river channel and lent mooring to boats of various size and description. The high tide mark was clearly visible as a dark straight line at the same height above the river on the curving line of poles. When the incoming waters were within a couple inches of the high tide mark and gradually slowed the upstream march, Davey would turn away from the float and slowly make his way out into the current. He didn't fight the current. As he made his way across the river, he just let it take him upstream in the narrowing boat channel. After swimming out into the river for a short distance he would turn his attention back to the crowd and signal with his hand to "come on." Usually a few of his stronger swimming friends would join in and share the experience. Sometimes Davey went alone. The enjoyment was achieved by giving in to the forces of nature. Sometimes the last of the incoming tide was strong enough to take them all the way up to the first bend in the river, almost a half mile upstream. However, usually it was somewhere in between. Then when the tide lay dormant then swirled and began its outward march to the sea, they would float and tread and paddle their way back down to the dock.

Winding its way a short distance through fruitful mulberry trees and thick laurel hillsides, the park road led to another favorite swimming spot, "Big Rock". This cove within the harbor is home to a small sandy beach which is guarded by a high, steep natural granite wall to the east and a prominent granite outeropping of smooth massive granite boulders which spring abruptly from the sand, to the west. This mass of rocks is capped off with one huge, flat rock (Big Rock) then descends on the opposite side of the beach in a shear drop to the water about twenty feet below. However the water at the base of "Big Rock" is surrounded by a circle of massive boulders, the circle being only about ten feet in diameter. Only the most daring of Davey's friends would make this jump. Davey wouldn't do it.

The bay then continues on to a larger crescent shaped muddier beach which is embraced by a high boulder studded cliff which reaches out with tall, proud defiance into the harbor. On the flat ground at the point of the cliff surrounded by gnarly twisted dwarf oaks that seemed equally defiant and tenacious, was a very large old abandoned vacation home. Thus this natural landmark shared its name with a manmade guest. The spot was known as "Castle Rock". On the flooding tide, Davey and his friends would swim across this bay and negotiate the steep climb up the steep boulder studded face, single file, to a flat rock which projected out over the water about thirty feet above. This was a great spot for high cliff diving as the water below was deep and harbored no obstacles.

Another choice was again very challenging. On the east flank of the small sandy beach, a short distance out on the curving granite wall is a very large flat smooth rock about twenty feet from the surface of the water. At the base of this sloping platform were boulders just below the surface of the water at high tide which projected out for a distance of about ten feet from the cliff. One couldn't dive from this spot, only take a good long run and jump from the edge in hopes of clearing the boulders and landing in the deep water beyond.

Davey never attempted this jump. He saw the bloody results of many jumps that never made it far enough. There seemed to be plenty of other ways to gain respect and admiration besides putting one's body or one's life for that matter, through such a risk.

So went the summer for a twelve year old energetic boy with long curly blonde hair and a new blue Schwinn banana seat bike and a chrome wheelie bar. It was a time for solitude. It was a time for crowded excitement when the big bluefish would invade the harbor. It was a time for watching and listening and learning and a special time and place to share. It seemed to Davey that nature provides everyone with a special place, a place that has the enchanting power to draw one back for more, time and time again.

Chapter 3
A Strong New Incoming

Undeniably, the seasons change and only with a fulfilled and enriched spirit from the past can one look to the future with a smile in their heart. After Labor Day school started up, and Davey's time spent at the Point was limited to evening and weekend adventures. The effects of shorter days and cooler nights were beginning to show. Instead of crowds of people and cars bringing noise and excitement, the harbor itself was beginning to intensify with natural seasonal changes.

Damp, hazy skies brought on winds drawn to shore by the heat of the land began to be taken over by dry, clear bright blue skies brought by winds born on land and drawn by the sea. It's a timeless time when one season resigns itself to another, a brief meeting, however more powerful and intimate then any mortal soul might begin to imagine. And every living part of that endless cycle in some sub-consciousness but instinctive manner, senses, and reacts to, and is part of, that unfathomable experience. And the tide is drawn highest into the marshes during the full moon closest to the fall equinox. The shinning rich brown sodden bank of soil and the shimmering green salt grass of the marsh draw the sea high and full into its bosom. And the sea eagerly engulfs everything it can reach. As the flood tide slackens, the ocean feeds the marsh with unseen richness. Then reluctantly the sea withdraws, pulling with it life to nurture the creatures of the sound. And both being fulfilled they separate to carry on their duties and eagerly await their next embrace.

During the first two weeks of September snapper blues become the greatest influence on the balance of life in the harbor. Many different species of small baitfish begin to school up close to shore, feeding heavily on the rich, microscopic plant and animal life that is drawn from the marshes by the outgoing tide, and pushed up into the salt grass with the flood. Relentlessly, with their keen sense of smell and vision and with suburb speed and stamina, the immature bluefish pursue their quarry, instinctively seeking to gorge themselves as full as possible. Instinctive knowledge tells them that as the waters quickly cool that they'll soon embark on their long, perilous voyage south for the winter. Marsh and shoreline locations become alive with fishermen and fishermen of birds and other creatures eager to take advantage of the annual slaughter. Voracious schools of these juvenile killing machines herd their prey to shore at every opportunity, providing a feast for themselves, the fishermen, the fishermen of birds, and an untold number of bottom dwelling creatures and microscopic forms of life that harvest every speck of protein during these events.

Towards the latter part of September the majority of this spectacle disappears into the vast openness of the sound, then out into the even greater expanse of the mighty Atlantic. Even as this event is winding down another even greater occurrence is arriving in the local waters. Huge schools of menhaden, a silvery foot long plankton feeding member of the herring family come through on their journey south and the mature bluefish take up their own relentless slaughter.

The screen door slowly creaked to a close. Joe sat in silence behind the main counter, his back to Davey. A dull yellow colored fishing rod spun between two sets of metal rollers with the constant pumping of Joe's foot on a small rubber covered metal pedal. Davey watched the man's hands as he worked different colored threads one at a time up above the long cork handle of the rod. Before long a beautiful diamond pattern began to emerge running half an arm's length up the blank from the end of the cork grip. Davey watched in silence, fascinated by the perfect geometric beauty being created with such simple means and equipment.

After completing that step on his new custom rod, Joe turned and greeted Davey. "The big ones are movin' in," he said, his brown eyes burning into Davey's with a shining squint. Joe took a long silent look at the boy, lowered his head then slowly brought it back up until their eyes met once more. Then he looked over to the corner by the front window. Davey followed Joe's glance which focused on a long, one piece fiberglass, cream colored rod with purple wrap holding the guides and tip. Attached to the rod with black electrical tape was a fairly large, sturdy looking grey spinning reel.

"Think you could handle that outfit Davey?" Joe asked as he continued to stare at the rod and reel leaning in the corner. "That's an eight foot Lamiglas medium action rod with a RuMer 602, perfect for shore fishing." Joe walked over to the corner, lifted the outfit up and over to the counter, placing it into Davey's outstretched hands. "It's nothing fancy but it'll sure get the job done," Joe announced in a quiet, confident tone.

Davey held the rod at arm's length, briskly jerking it up and down in order to get a feel for its action. The rod felt heavy and powerful and Davey thought to himself that there wasn't a fish that swam in the ocean that couldn't be brought to shore with this mighty piece of equipment.

"These big blues are some mighty powerful creatures," Joe advised Davey. They're pure energy with an unbelievable desire to multiply and survive. They're cagey too, smarter than most fish, and they'll do just about anything to maintain their freedom. Every one of them is different in its own struggle once that hook stings the side of its jaw. Every battle with one of these creatures is a unique and intimate experience.

Davey let on to Joe with a humble tone in his voice "I can't buy this outfit," Joe snapped back at Davey with an unusually stern tone to his voice, "I'll keep a tab for you, and you can pay me a little bit at a time." Davey looked up at Joe, his eyes filled with tears brought on by sheer joy and anticipation.

"Come on, let's rig it up," Joe continued reaching out and taking the rig from the boy's trembling hands. Joe then proceeded to remove the empty spool from the reel, drop it onto a home-made rolling device and fill it with twenty pound test "Ande Pink" monofilament line. "Don't ever want to fill it flush," Joe advised his young friend, "that causes too many tangles and you'll lose a lot of fishing time." Then Joe cut the line free, reattached the spool to the reel and strung the end of the line through the guides and eye tip and pulled an arm's length of line out beyond the tip. Then he proceeded to thread a small white nylon sleeve with a stainless steel snap attached to it up onto the line. Then he opened the snap, slid on a two ounce bank sinker and closed it back up. "Two ounces works from the rocks behind the Legion, three is better off the dock," Joe advised the boy. "See this rig allows a fish to pick up your bait and run line off the reel without feeling the unnatural weight of the sinker." Joe then proceeded to tie a two foot metal leader with an eight/0 stainless hook attached to it on the end of the line. "There now, you're all set. Just remember, after you cast out always watch your line where it enters the water. You'll see it moving towards shore as the sinker and bait settle to the bottom. When the line stops moving towards you, reel in the slack until there's a straight line from the tip of the rod to where it enters the water. Then pull the tip of the rod back until it's halfway between your head and the horizon. Then cradle the line with you forefinger just above the spool and flip the bail. When you feel a fish grab your bait, let the line go so the fish can run with it and hopefully swallow it. How long you wait before trying to set the hook is up to you. That's the beauty part of blue fishing. It's you and the fish. Sometimes they'll swallow the bait real quick and you'll hook'em deep down in the fullest, sometimes they'll just grab it and swim like hell towards midsound and run half your line off your reel in five seconds then just spit the bait out before you even have a chance to set the hook. That's one of the beauty parts of blue fishing Davey, it's never a guarantee, it's always a challenge, and there's no telling what the outcome is gonna be." Joe then disappeared into the back room and quickly returned, and placed a plastic bag with three fresh menhaden on the counter in front of Davey. He then grabbed a small heavy zip lock bag from under the counter and stuffed some extra leaders, hooks and fish-finder rigs inside. Then Joe pushed the bait and extra rigs to the front of the counter within Davey's easy reach.

"I'll put this on your tab," Joe said to his young friend. "Remember, pay attention, you'll only get so many chances if any at all every time you're there. Remember when you learn from your own experiences, success will be your reward."

Davey gathered up the extra gear and bait, brought it outside and put it down next to his bike. Then he went back inside. "Joe, I'll pay you, I get money. I cut lawns and I have a paper route in the morning with my brother," exclaimed the boy as he reached out to claim his powerful new tool.

Joe hesitated with his response but as the screen door creaked open announcing Davey's cautious departure Joe left him with some wise and well intended words. "Remember boy it's you and the fish, there's gonna be a lot of people out there that are gonna tell you how to catch them. If you try everything that they tell you to do and don't succeed, you might feel that they steered you wrong. Keep an open mind. Listen to the advice given from people that have experience, that's a good way to start. And remember that to be able to share with others, it takes a lot of time and experience of your own. Remember Davey, when you're ready, pull back hard three times and once for good luck, and your hook might just find a spot that holds fast."

Davey slowly coasted down to the dock. The sun had long past cleared the treetops above the southern arm of the bay. A lone fisherman was walking towards his truck, shoulders slumping downward from the weight of heavy bluefish that he clutched by the underside of the bony gill plate with each hand. Davey approached the stranger as he flipped the brace of fish onto the open tailgate of his pick-up. The boy watched in silent admiration while the fisherman cleaned his catch. "Nice fish," Davey said, breaking the silence.

"Yeah, they were in big-time, right at daybreak. They came in like a whirlwind of energy, smashing the bait right up to the beach. They had the menhaden packed in so tight, the water turned red with blood, they were so thick. Lots of people, lots of fish caught. Then as quick as they were here, they were gone."

Davey turned his attention away from what was going on close at hand. There was no one around, save for the seagulls which were spread out high above the shimmering waters of the bay intently scrutinizing its surface waiting for something to happen. Davey felt alone as he had hoped to show off his new fishing outfit to some of his friends. Suddenly he remembered what Joe had said to him earlier that morning. "It's just you and the fish," that's what Davey kept thinking to himself as he made his way up along the rocks behind the Legion, it's just you and the fish. However when he arrived at the flat on top of the rocks and looked out all around the beautiful harbor and far out into the open sound from this commanding viewpoint he thought to himself that maybe it wasn't just him and the fish and that Joe was only telling him part of it. "Looks like I'll have to learn how to do this on my own," Davey said to himself under his breath as he carefully maneuvered towards a flat spot on the rocks close to water's edge.

His first cast with the new outfit sailed far out into the bay. Davey felt impressed and satisfied with his effort as he sat down indian style and patiently set off on an awesome, challenging, brand new connection with the natural world around him.

Davey noticed that the outgoing tide had pushed the fish and the birds well offshore, out to the mouth of the harbor. There he could see birds circling and diving like rockets into scattered white foamy patches of baitfish, which in trying to escape the slaughter, were hurling themselves out of the water by the thousands in one quick sunlit flash after another. After watching the distant action for some time, Davey noticed small schools of menhaden breaking away from the huge dark mass of fins just breaking the surface. Slowly and deliberately, these smaller groups of fish were being herded towards shore at various locations within the bay. One fairly large school of these baitfish, perhaps an acre or so of tightly packed prey, swung around the outside edge of the town beach, and then headed directly towards the lone fisherman on the rocks. Before long the frenzy was right out in front of Davey. Panicked baitfish swam into his line, telegraphing their presence through it onto his trembling index finger curled around at the other end.

Then he felt the strike. It felt as if some unseen dynamic power had taken over. The line was wrenched away from his finger and peeled off of his reel with blinding speed. Davey watched in amazement as the amount of line of the spool rapidly decreased, then fearful there would soon be no line left to work with he stood up, closed the bail and pulled back hard. It felt as if he had snagged his hook onto a rock, or some other unmovable object on the ocean floor. Then he pulled back again and again then once more for good luck as Joe had instructed him to. Then he tried to reel, but the force at the other end was too strong. A very helpless and desperate feeling quickly welled up inside Davey. At this point he had all he could do to hold on and not let the fish either pull the pole from his hands or pull him into the water. Line continued to scream off of the reel and the pole itself seemed to be alive, dancing uncontrollably.

Suddenly, without warning or explanation, the line went slack and his pole assumed its natural straightness. "He's gone," Davey said out loud. Subconsciously he felt a great sense of relief as he began to reel in the weightless line. Then just when he thought he had gained it all back a long silver flash streaked past him, no more than ten feet out in the water from where he stood. Again line vanished from his reel and the rod dipped downward in a long bending arch. Then his line where it entered the water was quickly angling up, becoming level with the surface. Suddenly, not fifty feet out the fish exploded out of the water and into the air, violently shaking its head. Just before it dropped back into its natural environment, Davey saw the flash of his bait as it flew from the creatures snapping jaws. And he felt his line go slack again, but this time the fish was gone.

The boy's hands shook with adrenaline filled energy as he baited up again and made another long cast out into the middle of the boiling school of fish. Within minutes the line was racing in a blur from his spool once more. Again Davey drove the hook into the fishes' bony jaw. Again he was met with powerful resistance, however almost immediately this fish put on an acrobatic air borne display. It jumped and shook its head violently. It jumped and somersaulted back into the water. It jumped and tail walked across the top of the water launching the hook towards the rocks with a violent shake of its head, and was gone.

"How can anyone catch one of these things," Davey thought as he casted again. It seemed as if all the odds were in favor of the fish and that they were just playing a game. For a third time hook found flesh and Davey held on trying to reel, hoping that the fish would tire. This one though, felt even heavier and more powerful than the previous two that he had had on. This particular fish just headed straight out towards the mouth of the harbor, seemingly intent on getting as far away from shore in as short of time that was possible. Davey tightened down the anti-reverse knob on top of the spool in order to create greater resistance and hopefully slow the brute down but his line just kept peeling away at a fast, steady pace. So he took a chance and tightened the knob down as hard as he could. Immediately he was pulled to the edge of the rocks by an unbelievably powerful burst of energy. Then just when he thought he would either let the rod go and give it up to the sea, or hold on and get pulled off of the rocks and into the water, his line snapped with a loud merciful "pop". Davey tied on another rig and made another cast, but after an hour or so nothing else happened. The fish were gone. "Gone to God only knows where, on some uncharted reef in some unknown depths," he thought, looking out onto the vast shimmering expanse of blue.

Evening brought the promise of again connecting with the powerful and unpredictable bluefish. It also presented the opportunity to be part of a very profound seasonal spectacle. Towards sunset, the rocks behind the Legion would slowly become host to a small, intimate group of fishermen. Davey knew all of them having spent most of his free time in their presence as a youth. He felt welcome joining in their company and wanted badly to catch his first big bluefish among the people that he had watched and admired and shared in their success.

This was a group of fishermen that lived all year long with their memories of past fall experiences in anticipation of the possibility that the present one would be equally or greater enjoyed. So they filed in. Some of these people only fished in the fall, for big blues, from the rocks behind the Legion. Then there were people who fished as much as they could, for whatever was running. Then there were people that went out on their boats at first light, and fished until the ten-o-clock morning breeze ushered them back into the harbor, that showed up to join their comrades. To a man, it seemed as if they were drawn in the evening by some unknown force down to the rocks behind the Legion as if nature had intended them to participate in this experience and have the opportunity to pass it along, if they so chose to do so.

So they took up their positions and sat and looked out over the bay, and waited in silence carefully checking their gear making sure that everything was in order. Then they'd bait up and cast out, and look out over the bay, and out into the darkening waters of the sound, and patiently wait for something to happen. A special and much welcomed part of this event was that the old time commercial fishermen were a part of it. They enjoyed coming down just to relax and reminisce and enjoy each other's company, even though they saw each other almost daily but at a distance as they worked the waters of the sound. And, Davey thought that part of the reason that they came down was to simply catch a fish with rod and reel.

Among these old weathered veterans there was Brooksie. He was a tall fair, skinned man with long arms and legs and an equally long head which harbored a perfect set of long ivory-looking teeth. His eyes were as blue as the sky on a clear crisp autumn day and were encased by deeply wrinkled skin that tightened up, wrinkles growing deeper with his smile. Then there was Louie "the cigar man". His nickname originated from the fact that his family owned a considerable amount of stock in a popular Connecticut Broad Leaf cigar company. Louie was a short, wiry and powerful man. He had a balding, short white hairline, and a face that was as red as a cooked lobster. Another constant figure on the rocks in the fall was Fresco. He was short and stocky and bald with only a handful of teeth remaining in his weathered leather-like jaws. Fresco was the most outgoing, sharing, youthful, energetic member of the old time commercial fishermen's group. Then there was Albie, who never talked loud enough to be heard by more than one person at a time. But when Albie talked, his words always held real meaning and purpose and were always very truthful. It usually took a physical effort on the part of the person that Albie was talking to in order to accept his wisdom for reality.

This group of fishermen was given the most respect from all the others. They had their traditional fishing spots on the rocks and no one occupied their spot unless they didn't come down till twilight had set in. Even if someone showed up that wasn't aware of this procedure, and tried to settle into one of these "reserved spots" it was made clear to him that if the rightful occupier of this "throne" was to show up he would be told in a subtle and polite manner, with the acknowledgment of everyone present, to concede that location.

So that's the way it was. The old timers were respectfully granted their designated spots. That seemed to make everything right, and to establish an unspoken connection amongst the entire group of fishermen. Then after everyone had settled down, fishing became their priority.

Sunset gave way to darkness in a world of ever dimming light. Everyone and everything seemed to radiate the mellow, calm energy given off by the last rays of the sun as it dipped below the horizon and lit up the sky with fiery brilliance. The harbor was full of life, and the struggle to stay alive. And the fishermen on the rocks had been drawn there by some unconscious, primo real instinct to be part of that drama. To be connected with the whole experience by a thin strand of monofilament seemed to instill a sense of separation from any other thoughts or concerns.

With the onsought of the first evening stars beginning to sparkle in the paling sky the fish came into shore, acres and acres of swirling, boiling, foaming fury. And people caught fish. And people lost fish. And the excitement was felt by everyone.

Then it grew dark, and an oil burning lantern would go on for a few minutes then be shut off so that everyone could re-adjust their vision to the natural state at hand. People brought lanterns down for the purpose of re-baiting a hook or unhooking a fish, or to shed some close light to help land a fish, but mostly it was just the natural light of the moon and stars, and the occasional iridescent flashes in the water, caused by thousands of small, clear, invisible jellyfish as they came in contact with any foreign object such as one's line where it entered the water.

Davey was totally focused on the pressure of the line gripped in his forefinger. He could feel every subtle movement of the tide as it pulsed strong then slow, strong then slow, like the breath entering then leaving his own body. The he felt something grab his offering and could actually feel the fish biting the bait and shaking its head in an attempt to remove it from the hooks grasp. The boy waited a long time before he felt confident that the fish had taken his bait in earnest. The he slowly stood up and pulled back hard, three times and one for good luck.

"He's on," Davey announced with excitement. Now he thought that this was his big chance. Everyone was there. The fish ran but the young lad applied just enough pressure, and kept his concentration, and managed to turn it back towards the shore. He kept the pressure on, pulling back then reeling down as he had witnessed so many times before. "That's it boy, good job keep it up don't give him any slack," Whitey encouraged him in a calm tone of voice.

So with everyone present, and with Davey being the focus of everyone's attention he felt like the biggest, most important person in the whole world.

Then he was down on the landing rock and the fish was close and Whitey was close with a lantern and gaff. And the whole world was right there, in the small dim light shining on the rock, the seaweed swaying with the tide, and this big, beautiful fish, so full of energy and resilience came shaking and sparkling and bleeding out of the water at the end of Whitey's gaff.

Bluefish season was drawing to a close. Late October brought the promise of shorter days and colder nights. With one or two Nor-Easters, gone would be that exhilarating time of year. And those who had shared the experience had become richer and content inside. In the evenings they gathered, not just to fish, but to talk, and share stories and share some very special and personal times.

Most people had gardens back then, and at this special time of year the fruits of their labor were traditionally shared. And the old time commercial fishermen would share and exchange some of their specialties. Albie would bring pickled herring, caught and processed on his own. Brooksie made a clam chowder that could be matched by no-one. The cigar man had a way with a lobster bisque. And on and on it went, people sharing their own personal harvest among themselves in a very simple, respectful traditional manner. So that's how it went for Davey, for those years, with his blue Schwinn bike and his eight foot Lamiglas pole with the purple wrap and Rumer reel.

Chapter 4
The Inside Passage

The boat had been resting upside down for years. It laid alongside a rusty page metal fence nearly unnoticeable, due to the weeds and brush that had grown around and over it. It was Davey's great uncle's boat, whom had passed away when Davey was very young. Davey had never given any thought in regards to checking out its condition, he had always assumed that due to the length of time that it had gone unattended, there was probably not much hope of reconstruction.

In the spring of his sixteenth year, Davey got a feeling that it was worth checking it out. So along with a couple of his friends, they took some planks and flipped the paint peeled hull over. To their astonishment, they discovered that the inside of the sixteen foot fiberglass runabout was quite well preserved. This they thought, was probably due to the fact that she had been resting on heavy timbers, which allowed for proper ventilation and kept it away from contact with the ever eager decomposing elements held within the soil.

Topsides there were two molded fiberglass seats facing the dashboard. The bow was enclosed, and curled slightly upward from the gunwales back from the stern for a distance of about six feet. This provided an area for easily accessible dry storage. Two seats faced the stern, molded into the ones that faced the bow. Behind those seats was an open deck that was probably six feet long and five feet wide. She had a fairly high freeboard capped off with a six inch wide rub rail. Her interior was a flat powder blue, the shade not unlike that of a clear, dry mid-day May sky.

When Davey saw that the boat had the potential to be brought back into seaworthy condition, he raced to his house to confide with his parents. They agreed that he could assume responsibility for the craft only after the O.K. was given by its handed down owner uncle Jack.

Uncle Jack was fine with the idea, so now Davey owned a boat, well just the hull of a boat really. He honestly didn't know where to begin the task of making her shipshape and seaworthy so he hopped on his bike and set off to see Albie.

Davey considered Albie a person that possessed supernatural knowledge in regards to boats and fishing and everything that had to do with the water and everything that was connected with it. He found his friend in his backyard, sitting on an upside down five gallon pail, scrutinizing one of his old homemade wooden lobster traps, which was sitting on top of a brand new one. Davey pulled up next to him and watched in silence as Albie nimbly mended a small break in the front nylon entry net

Without taking his focus from the task in which he was presently carefully and patiently attending to, Albie began to speak to the boy. "You know them two long antennas that stick out of their heads? That's like their brain boy, like an extension of their primitive simple yet very effective means of survival. It's their way over millions and millions of years, to be able to know in basic yet intimate detail whatever form of foreign or familiar dead or living space filling matter that they encounter. Ah if we all could be that fortunate to have some physical attachment on our bodies that gave our minds the power to know the answers to life's unending and mysterious questions.

See this broken mesh I'm mending? Even before a lobster goes into this trap, it would already have figured a way to get back out. If I'm gonna invest the time and effort and expense, my traps are gonna hold any keeper lobster that ventures its way in.

Otherwise I'm just feeding them.

"Anyhow, what brings you to this so rarely seen neck of the woods?" Albie asked, taking his attention from his now completed task. "I want to fix up my great uncle John's boat," Davey replied. "But I really don't know where to start. I was thinking that maybe you could come over and check it out and give me some advice. I know that you're really busy getting all of you traps and lines and buoys and nets in order for the spring, but I'd really appreciate if you could just come over and point me in the right direction."

"Is that the boat with the powder blue finish and the high gunwale and the back to back fiberglass seats?" Albie asked his young friend.

"Yeah that's it," Davey replied, "and it seems to still be in pretty good shape too."

"Alright lad, you be on your way and I'll see you in a little while."

"Yeah, John loved to fish," Albie reflected as he slowly walked over to the boy whom was standing proudly inside of his not so new vessel. "I remember him out on the sound. He knew the spots. He loved his black fishing, and he was good at it because he put his time in. Hell, I remember when we were kids we used to row out to the Beacon and catch bushels of blackfish in the fall, and the way home was even more difficult with a boatload of fish. When you put your time into something that you really want, and you're patient and willing to accept the fact that the whole experience in achieving your goal is a unique learning and growing experience, shared with everything in your presence as it is sharing with you, only then will you be truly rewarded."

"Yeah she weathered all of those years pretty well, but the first thing that you have to do is turn her upside down again and apply a heavy coat of fiberglass cloth all the way up to and beyond the waterline and finish it off with three coats of resin. Then maybe all those old seams will hold water. Then you could put a coat of bottom paint on her and flip her back over but just make sure that you keep her up off the ground. " Davey followed Albie's instructions and in a few weeks time, his boat was ready for the water, Harry Johnson owned a boat dealership not far from Davey's house. He also owned a small marina behind his house, on Harbor street, on the Branford river, which was less than a mile from Davey's house. Davey needed stuff, lots of stuff in order to make his dream a reality. Harry was an old yankee who was very conscientious regarding the fact that if something had the possibility of being recycled, and one had the space to hang on to it then hang on to it. Harry had stored more used boating equipment in every nook and cranny in his long, narrow, dilapidated warehouse than seemingly anyone east of the Mississippi.

So Harry was Davey's main man, and he steamed over to his establishment and entered into a place that was equally filled with old and new boats and motors and equipment and accessories. Harry took a liking to Davey's quiet fascination, and provided him with very functional second hand equipment with which he needed to make his boat functional. He produced an old fiberglass Atwood steering wheel; some used nylon rollers for the steering cable, used running lights, an old danforth anchor with rope, old wooden oars, and life jackets and most importantly of all a nineteen-sixty-four, twenty eight horsepower two cylinder outboard motor with controls and cables, for the mere sum of four hundred dollars.

Albie was always there with advice and coached Davey through the project of installing all of the equipment and gave his nod of approval with a twinkle in his eye when she was finally ready for her rebirth.

Now Davey needed a place to moor his dream come true. With his savings nearly depleted, he thought again about Harry and that maybe he could help Davey out. He knew that it was his only affordable option regarding a slip judging by the broken down appearance of Harry's marina which Davey had observed countless times on his journeys to and from the harbor.

"I'll work for it," Davey announced in an honest and positive tone. "Summer vacation is only a month away, and anyways I want to learn all that I can about boats and engines and the water, and I want to go fishing." Harry paused for a long moment before responding, his clouded ancient blue eyes staring deeply into the clear, bright energetic blue eyes of a young boy that was longing to open a door into a mysterious and challenging world.

"Well, I have one inside slip still open on the north side of the ramp," Harry announced. "Not much water in a moon tide, but it's a slip none the less and only two hundred and fifty dollars for the season, which runs from April fifteenth to November fifteenth. My wife Abby takes care of the bookwork, so first chance you get, go down and give her a deposit and we'll work the rest out after that".

That Saturday morning, Davey made his way down to Johnson's marina and gave Abby some money towards his slip. "Its slip 'H'," Abby announced to the excited young lad. After writing down some basic information in an ancient paperback journal, Abby told Davey that he was welcome to go down and check out the dock and his slip.

Past the dirt parking area, the landscape gave way to a beautiful expanse of lime green marsh grass up and down the river. It was less than a hundred feet wide on the bank where Davey stood, due to the fact that there were homes and other marinas lining the western shore. However the eastern bank rose up into an expansive undeveloped marsh. It seemed like a quiet, peaceful place. The decaying condition of the unpainted planks on the ramp and piers, and the straight, tall narrow trees that held the whole mass in place, seemed to fit right into the landscape, unlike the other massive, commercially developed marinas clustered much further downstream.

Standing at the end of the long, tall main pier, Davey took the time to focus on everything that surrounded him. He noticed that the tide ran strong in the narrow channel. He saw the wind gently swaying the green marsh grass. He became familiar with the small group of boats that were nestled together, swaying ever so gently back and forth in the river's current, along both sides of the floats which projected at right angles from the base of the steep gangplank. "Seems safe and secure," Davey said out loud to himself, far enough up-river, away from the sound's stormy wrath. "It's a good spot, a really good spot."

Make sure that she's in neutral, push the throttle lever all the way forward then pull it back to half, pull out the choke knob then pull that starter cord with all you got boy." Davey's boat was nestled within the high long narrow wooden confines of the state launching ramp on the Branford river. Albie had trailored it down for him on a mid-Saturday morning in late May. Davey followed Albie's instructions; however, after three hard pulls on the starter cord, no life came from the motor. "Push the choke in, she's probably got enough gas now." Davey pushed the lever in and with one quick heave on the starter cord; the old little two cylinder sprang to life.

"Now get back to the helm and slowly idle her down lad," Albie said with a distinctive tone of excitement in his voice. "If she starts to stall, give her a little more gas, you'll get the feel of it after a while; she'll become like a part of you. Just focus on how she sounds all the time. When you're out on the sound, she's gonna be your best, most intimate friend so pay attention to that methodical unbroken hum. Always keep the sound of that rhythm in the front of your consciousness, that's your link back to shore. If there's ever any skip or hesitation or strange sound coming from that motor, make a bee-line towards the nearest shore then work your way back into the harbor. Remember, the nearest shore first, then the harbor. Good luck, pay attention, I'll be watching out for you when I see you out there." And with that being said, and the motor purring steadily, Albie was gone.

Davey slowly backed out from the confines of the ramp and into the quietly flowing realm of the river. Its outgoing tide immediately took hold of the small, heavy vessel, quickly pulling her downstream, her bow facing the near shore and her stern facing the far. Davey reacted quickly and instinctively, putting her in forward and coming about in a graceful fluid motion. He slowly eased the vessel into the middle of the channel, and then proceeded proudly and confidently upstream the quarter of a mile, to Johnson's marina.

Daybreak on the following morning held no wind and a clear sky. As the motor warmed up to running temperature, Davey took the time to make sure that everything was in order. His initial apprehension was slowly being replaced with an awareness that no matter how much he'd dwelt on the physical capabilities of his equipment, this journey would be the first into a new dimension of his life. There would be a world of adventure and opportunities opening up to him, so in order to make the best of it, he figured he'd better pay attention.

Halfway downstream to the state ramp, a strange feeling came over Davey. He turned the boat around and headed back upstream way up, past his dock, past the last few remaining small marinas, then under the Indian Neck bridge.

This is a low, two lane bridge, with two narrow channels separated by a series of large round concrete columns which form the foundation for the main upper support of the bridge. On the upstream side of the bridge the river opens up into a long, wide shallow mud flat with enough water from mid-tide and up to safely accommodate small outboard vessels. As a matter of fact, the bridge marks the end of the maintained channel and therefore the six mile per hour speed limit was not in effect on the other side.

The little twenty-eight horsepower motor labored for a moment when Davey put her up to three quarter throttle, but soon planed the heavy old hull off nicely and achieved a comfortable cruising speed. Davey was happily impressed with her performance.

He had never been in control of anything with such mechanical power. He cruised around up above the bridge for awhile, gaining confidence and getting a feel for how the boat handled. Then he headed back downstream, down past Mill creek and the state ramp to the last bend and into the straightaway leading to the town dock. He passed the dock and followed the channel out toward the mermaids. Once through the channel between the two small islands, he was overwhelmed by the vastness of the open sound. Just past the mermaids, a sudden unexplained fear overcame the boy and he turned the boat around and headed back into the relative safety of the harbor. Then just before he got to the dock, he turned her around again and steamed out without looking back.

Passing Johnson's point, the boulder strewn western extremity of Branford harbor, Davey put the boat in neutral and took out a map that he had studied so many times on shore but never from out on a the water. He took note of the different colored marker buoys within eyesight and referred to them on his chart. Then he headed in a southeasterly direction out past Taunton rock, a narrow island about a quarter-mile long made up of large, white, sun-bleached boulders that surround a lush green interior of low marsh grass. And upon continuing on his present course, the entire shoreline of Branford, and points beyond to the east and west slowly became exposed to view.

Again Davey put the boat in neutral and this time he shut off the motor. He had never before seen the world from this perspective. Everything around him that was natural: the sound, which seemed to be moving as one unified body of water in its outgoing flow to the sea, the islands within view that sprung from the water in various shapes and sizes just offshore. And the diversified characteristics of the shoreline itself brought to Davey an overwhelming feeling of unbounded freedom.

Then out of nowhere a stiff, chilly ocean breeze sprang up and awoke Davey from his dreamlike state. Within minutes the darkening water rose into a fairly large swell marching ponderously towards shore, capped with an ever increasing amount of foamy white crests. The little boat, heavy as she was, rode the valleys and crests of the swells quite nicely without rocking much at all, until Davey started her up and put her to the task of getting him home. Now natural energy met man made energy and Davey was suddenly in a situation that made him feel all alone, like he was the only person on earth. And that bright, sunny, peaceful summer shoreline now looked so very far away.

He remembered what Albie had told him weeks earlier, that at the first signs of trouble or if he started to feel uncomfortable, to head for the safety of the nearest shore then make his way back to the harbor. But Davey didn't know the safe routes along the rock and reef strewn shoreline. So he headed toward the low boxlike silver and green tower atop the big mermaid, about two miles away. In trying to hold a direct course towards the tower he was going right into the swells and the little boat plowed hard into the middle of every swell achieving only a few seconds of freedom before being pushed into the one ahead. Davey steered the boat away from his direct course and began to quarter into the waves. The resistance was broken and a much more natural flow took over. The boat angled smoothly up and over each swell, riding down into the valley with its force and up and over and into the next one. "Yeah," Davey exclaimed out loud. It'll take a little longer to get there but man, now I'm back in control. So he got in and on the way he learned a lot. He learned how to watch each swell and got the feel of how to steer slightly into it to meet it and become a part of its energy, natural energy and manmade energy moving in rhythm towards the same destination.

"You gotta learn the inside passage," Albie said to Davey in a quiet but very serious tone. "I was out there the other morning. I was watching out for you. I saw how you first fought the sea in your struggle to reach the safety of the harbor and how you adjusted your course and became one with it. You did a great job with it, but what you didn't see was the darkening of the water in the oncoming sea breeze. What you didn't smell was the smell of all of that non-native sea life caught up in the wind that came to share it with us. Watch the clouds, watch the tide, watch the water, and someday you'll understand that they're all connected and how that one thing leads to another in the natural order. But if you learn the inside passage, you'll have the ability to control your destination, and not be controlled by the forces of nature."

Albie was referring to the inside waterway from Jeffery point on the east side of the outer harbor to the Thimble islands and points beyond, as well as the stretch of shoreline from Johnson's point on the west side of the outer harbor that ran down to the Farm river and beyond to New Haven harbor. This area of the shoreline is sheltered from rough or stormy conditions on the main body of the sound by an intricate stretch of islands and reefs and rocks that lie just offshore.

"Study your chart. Go first on a dead low tide when most of the hidden dangers lie bare and naked. Also focus on the other potential places of trouble like sandbars and rocks and reefs that don't go awash, even on the ebb and even things uncharted. Then go at high tide and mark the difference, and don't try to remember all that you saw the first time. Don't go too far all at once, for to learn about the inside passage you must learn more than just the rocks and reefs and sandbars but also the wind and tide itself. You could learn as much as you want or as little as you want, but even in your whole lifetime, no matter how much you fall in love with the sea, there will always be challenges and mysteries to unlock. That's the beauty of a life on the water."

So Davey spent that whole summer trying to become intimately familiar with the local shoreline. He marked Albie's advice well. One trip would be at dead low tide, and the next would be on the flood. He would only venture a little further each time, making sure to remember all of the dangerous spots that he had learned on his previous trips. He realized that it was still possible to be out on the sound even when the sea on the outside was dark and angry because the inside passage provided a relatively safe calm environment with innumerable possibilities. As his trips took him further and further from the harbor a strong sense of confidence and freedom began to take over his perception of all the potential experiences that were being presented in the realm of the inside passage.

He didn't fish that whole summer. Instead, Davey just learned the water. He learned how the tide in the sound traveled in a big circle. The flow came into the sound from the east running strongest along the southern edges of the islands and rocks and reefs and generally stronger out towards mid-sound. And with the outgoing it seemed to swing more towards the shoreline and run strongest along the northern edges of all the natural physical elements in its way. And he learned that the wind and tide are bound together as one. He saw that when the tide changed so did the wind. It seemed to him that if the wind was building just before a change of tide that it would become even stronger with the turn. And if the wind was dying down just before the tide turned, more often than not, there would be calm seas for at least the first few hours of the new tide. Then during mid-tide when everything is moving with its greatest intensity, there seemed to be a time when the wind came up with the idea of changing directions. So even when the water was calm and the tide was slack it was like the next tide would bring an ever evolving circle of somewhat predictable events.

Davey's love for the sound grew stronger with each trip, and his boat was his link to a whole different world. He explored islands, he landed on sandy beaches, he came into port at different spots along the shoreline to refuel or get something to eat, or just hangout for awhile and enjoy the foreign shoreline from a land based perspective. Then after what seemed like a long unending blissful dream, it was Labor Day weekend, the end of summer and back to a school routine.

Davey still had the weekends to enjoy boating on the sound; however the early morning calm and the warm midday breezes that he had come to count on were coming to an end. The weather became unpredictable as if summer was struggling to hold on, and fall was beginning to make its presence known. "When the dry northwest winds of fall push out the warm tropical breezes of summer, everything that migrates north in the warm currents gather with the retreating force and together begin their long journey southward. Albie was trying to explain to Davey about the changes that occur in the sound from summer to fall. "Now the sound is full of life that has an instinctive goal to move with its summer bounty. A deliberate frenzy overcomes those creatures that must now travel hundreds of miles before settling down again in their primordial winter grounds. Even those creatures that are native to the sound will react to the shorter days and cooling water temperatures. Everything changes from one season to the other. You talk like you know the sound, like you have power over it, like you could predict its next move and defy or overcome anything that it presents to you. Yeah, summer weather is pretty predictable, but in the fall it's a whole different ball game."

"But now it's totally different out on the sound. You talk of the wind and the tide, but what of the clouds? In the fall more than any time of year, keep your eye on the clouds. Watch the sky to the northwest and when you see those big bright puffy white balloons appear on the horizon you got about two hours if you're lucky to get in, depending on the stage of the moon and tide. Be careful in the fall when you're out on the sound, the northwest wind has no mercy, and when it comes up on the start of an incoming tide, and you're any distance offshore, when you get back you'll have known its wrath."

The big bluefish had schooled up in earnest throughout the sound by mid-September, and Davey started fishing. It didn't seem to matter where he went once he got out of the harbor and out into the open sound, there were schools of bluefish feeding on huge masses of menhaden almost anywhere that he looked. Even though a fish or two could be caught by chasing the ever moving activity of predation, Davey came to enjoy just anchoring up and fishing on the bottom with fresh chunks of menhaden. When fishing in such a manner he could relax and take in the whole experience.

And in this experience he reflected on a message that his friend Albie had left with him one late evening as he departed from the rocks behind the legion.

"Be patient; let your thoughts be like a river within you, flowing freely through the ocean of your mind. When you experience something, think of it as an incoming tide. You have the chance to learn and grow fuller, like the water rising in the marsh. Try to understand that everything around you, if you look close enough, is constantly changing and never the same. Try to understand how these changes affect everything that is part of them. If you get out of focus in any situation in your life, look at something very close to you. Take a minute and just concentrate on that one close thing. What color is it? Is it alive, dead, moving, still? Where did it come from? What purpose does it have in this world? Then go back to what was unclear and you'll see it in a different light. And when you don't understand why something happened, let your mind be like the stillness of the slack tide. Sometimes it'll take a couple tides or even a couple days' tides to put it all together, but if you let your mind flow freely like the river, it will come to you. And when it does, you'll feel more a part of being alive. And there were plenty of fish, and he started taking his friends to share the experience.

It was an early Saturday evening with an ebbing tide, clear skies, and a light breeze when Davey ventured out to the east with three of his friends. This was an unusually large group for his small boat, as he felt more comfortable with only one passenger. However in the excitement of the tremendous fall bluefish run, and with seemingly ideal conditions, Davey had given in to the regards of his three friends and agreed to take them along.

Davey knew a good spot to the east. It's a small reef about a half a mile offshore with a deep channel with a strong current just along its southern edge. He knew from experience that the big blues cruised through that channel whenever the tide was running strong. The reef lies about four miles from the mouth of Branford harbor. For about three quarters of that distance, Davey was familiar with the inside passage and he navigated along its route through that reach, however when unfamiliar waters laid ahead, he changed course and steamed south out into the open sound.

The anchor found its hold and the baits were lowered to the bottom. Almost immediately the fish began to hit, the four boys were experiencing the most unbelievable fishing trip that any of them had ever experienced. At any given moment someone had a fish on. Sometimes they all had a fish on at the same time. The bottom of the boat was quickly becoming covered with fish and scales and blood.

Although the steady action that the boys were caught up in didn't change, other things were. It was getting dark and it was nearly a full moon that lit the darkening horizon and the tide was about to turn. Davey didn't notice the long, heavy dark line of balloon clouds quickly advancing towards them that loomed low in the western sky. He didn't acknowledge the freshening breeze on his face. He didn't notice that the seas were beginning to build and that the water to the west was growing darker and darker with the stiffening wind. It was only when the building waves and changing tide wrestled the anchor from its hold on the bottom and put them adrift, that Davey put their present situation into prospective.

"Reel-up, Davey announced firmly, loud enough to get everyone's attention however not trying to display any feeling of panic in his voice. He fired up the engine and in the darkening sky calmly pulled in the anchor and stowed it under the bow.

By now the seas had built to four-feet high, and the west wind was blowing at a steady twenty knots. Davey began the long journey back to the harbor. He could only keep the boat directly into the wind and swells as he didn't dare head toward shore as he wasn't familiar with that reach of the inside passage. Now it was quickly growing dark and the boat began to take on water. They were taking on water over the bow with every wave. His three friends bailed constantly, with frantic looks in their eyes.

"A little further and we'll cut inside," Davey announced calmly to his friends. "I can see the Brown's reef bell. Once we get by that we're home free," he assured them in a confident tone. And he made the bell. Then he began to quarter into the waves and the boat no longer had to proceed directly into the elements.

As Davey began to maneuver his vessel in a more natural flow with the elements, everyone breathed a sigh of relief. Now he realized how close they had come to not making it back in. He was quite sure that he would not be looking at the welcome sight of the flashing light on the big mermaid had he not known the shoreline route. They most certainly would have gone down.

It seemed as if everyone just kept their thoughts to themselves back on shore. However, Davey was pretty sure that they all were saying thanks to whatever power or powers that brought them safely back from that unforgettable trip.

The next morning Davey went down to check on his boat. It had sunk overnight at its mooring. He was quite upset to say the least but just being alive and safe on shore made the tragedy seem very easy to overcome. And it also seemed to the young lad that he had learned a very important lesson.

Chapter 5

The Codfather

It seems as if nature provides everyone with a special place, a place to be alone yet a part of and enriched by everything around them.

Late in the spring of the following year, Davey got another boat. It was an old wooden sixteen-footer with a nice high freeboard and a small homemade hardtop with a fixed plexiglas window on either side of two in the front. The price was right as it was given to him by the father of a friend, with the agreement that if Bobby and Davey fixed it up they would be mutual owners.

She needed some work. The screws that held the keel onto the bottom of the boat were completely rusted away and the transom had a fair amount of dry rot, making it questionable as to how well it would hold up under the strain and vibration created by an outboard motor big enough to adequately propel her. Fortunately Bobby's father was an old Swedish craftsman and he had agreed to help the boys restore the boat.

So off came the keel. Then they sanded both sides of the seam underneath and put three coats of fiberglass cloth and resin from stem to stern in an eight inch wide strip. Then they sanded the oak keel smooth and screwed it back on with three inch brass screws which they spaced every ten inches or so. Then they put another coat of resin over it to bond it with their patch underneath.

With that being done it was time to address the transom issue. Bobby's father came to the conclusion that they should completely replace it. They cut off the old one and also removed the last set of ribs at the end of the hull that had been connected to it. After making up two new ribs and fastening them on either side with screws and epoxy resin, they designed and built and applied a new double three-quarter inch plywood transom.

Bobby's father was thorough. He thought things out before he set forth to his task. Davey and Bobby both got a lot of satisfaction working with the old man, and also learned the importance of being patient, developing a game plan for the job ahead of you, being confident with it and then executing the job in an orderly manner. Then they painted the bottom, flipped her back over, reattached the cabin, painted everything and she was ready.

Now what about a motor? Well fortunately Davey's parents had made him take out a three-hundred dollar insurance policy on his first boat and the old twenty-eight horsepower Johnson had been completely rebuilt and was standing ready in the old wooden rack, behind the old picture window in Harry Johnson's old broken down boat and motor dealership and repair service.

Harry helped the boys out with an old shift box and control cables, an old steering wheel with a new cable, and anchor, lines, oars, cleats, life jackets, running lights and a fire extinguisher. All of this equipment went on Davey's account and assured Harry that Davey would be spending a good part of the next two summers paying it off by helping him out at the store and marina.

And off they went. Davey was back out on the open sound. It was summertime again; school was out and with a new cabin boat and rebuilt motor, the seventeen year-old lad felt like he was on top of the world.

Bobby however soon became bored with the boat. He had a car and he was a few years older than Davey, and he had older friends. So the boat and bills and responsibilities that came with it just kinda became Davey's. Towards the middle of the summer, Davey was beginning to lose interest in the boat himself. Going out mostly by himself, and many times fishing for hours without even getting a bite was becoming a bit monotonous.

Then one midmorning as he was on his way in from another fairly unsuccessful fishing trip, he noticed that a sizeable crowd had gathered on the town float and a small open wooden boat was tied alongside. Davey pulled up to the float at right angles to the other vessel and tied off.

A hefty, burly young man, dressed in full heavy duty foul weather fishing gear stood amidships, covered with scales and blood and dripping jellyfish surrounded by a somewhat organized chaos.

In the bow lay a large monofilament gillnet. Behind that were two wooden fish boxes full of shiny scaly fish of various sizes and species. Behind the center counsel and the heavily bearded fisherman with a round red face and long wildly curled brown hair was a stack of wooden lobster pots against either side of the gunwale and in-between them were two metal wire bushel baskets full of lobsters covered with a fresh layer of wet seaweed.

On the starboard side of the vessel, from amid ships running down to the stern was an oak culling board about twelve inches wide attached to the gunwale. Ahead of that was a round arched metal davit. Presently a small scale with a galvanized tray held on by three light chains, was attached to the davit. In a simple way, and with basic means, the fisherman had brought his store to a group of people eager for some fresh seafood, and a wide variety at that. Lobsters went on the scale, then into a brown bag and then into the hands of some happy customer. Then conch, then bluefish then butterfish, weaks, sea robins, and even sand sharks graced that metal tray. Davey couldn't believe the abundance and variety of fish and shellfish that this man had harvested in apparently half a morning's effort.

The breeze had picked up and Davey listened to the rhythmic sound of waves as they caressed the sand on the town beach.

A building swell gently lifted and lowered his boat along with the float and everyone on it. The bright midmorning sunshine glistened on the surface of the river and everything around him seemed to be so alive. To add to the contentment of the moment, a baitfish was being cut up into small pieces by the fishermen, and cast out one at a time to a formidable sized flock of gulls that were lingering around carefully looking for the opportunity to grab an easy meal. The fishermen let out a loud deep hearty chuckle as he proceeded to work the birds into a screeching diving, flying and fighting frenzy. Then when the last customer had made his way up the short metal gangplank to the parking lot, the carefree captain fired up the small engine, untied his scarred up little wooden skiff, and with a tip of his worn out duck-billed canvas hat, and with a mellow grin in his eyes and mouth, pulled away from the float and slowly made his way upriver giving his boat a little fishtail as he crossed over to the far side of the channel.

Davey just sat there for awhile, trying to put the whole event into perspective. He knew that Albie was a commercial fisherman along with Brooksie and the Cigar Man. However these reclusive old timers never stopped at the town float. They always just sort of snuck out before first light and then snuck back in with their catches being well concealed. This was the first time that Davey had been exposed to the diversified bounty that the sound had to offer. He got out of his boat and scurried up the gangplank. Several men were still hanging around their pick-up trucks talking. Davey approached the group and asked, "Who was that fisherman down on the float?" A short old man with a small build and white hair replied, "That my boy was the Codfather." "Where does he keep his boat?" the boy asked. "Way upriver, behind the old factory," the old man replied.

Davey wanted to meet this fisherman and maybe learn a little as to what this commercial fishing deal was all about. Unfortunately a feeling of apprehension came over him when he considered the fact that he had one more year left in high school and that he still owed Harry Johnson a lot of money for his slip and all of the boat equipment that he had bought on credit.

Throughout that summer and fall, Davey kept an eye out for that little green beat-up wooden boat. He took note of where the fisherman set out his gillnet and how he moved his lobster traps around from reef to mud then back to reef again. He seemed to be able to see the activity under water all the way down to the bottom.

One afternoon, Davey decided to go and visit his friend Albie. As usual he was sitting on a five gallon pail in the shade behind his house studying the top lobster trap of a two trap stack. He wasn't working on the trap, only staring at it as if he and it were having some kind of silent conversation or meeting. Albie looked up at the boy half startled upon sensing his presence. "What brings you around these parts? Why aren't you off running around with your buddies, or out on your boat?" Albie asked.

"Well Albie, it's getting kind of boring out on the boat," Davey replied. "The fishing's been terrible, and to tell you the truth I got a year of school left and was thinking maybe after that, I'd like to try some commercial fishing."

"Ahhhh," Albie let out a long, deep sigh. "So you want to be a commercial fisherman, and do you know why? Don't answer me, I'll tell you why. Because it's free, you're a free spirit, you love the water and you want to control your own destiny. You don't want to punch a time clock or have to answer to anyone, only the wind and the tide and the waves. Now tell me how close was I to your answer?"

"You know Albie, I just thought of it as being a fun way to make a living but what you just said was absolutely right."

"Well boy let me tell you something, making a living off the water is like farming, but it's a lot harder. Your nets and traps are like seeds being cast out into a vast and mysterious garden, a garden with ever changing lifeblood. And you're thinking that it's an easy blissful way of life, you're totally wrong. It takes a long time and a lot of hard work and dedication and perseverance in order to understand how and why things change out in the sound and how to anticipate these changes to be successful."

Davey took his friend's words to heart and thought about their conversation often, and his last year of high school flew by in what seemed like one long anticipated exhale of a deep, deep breath. Now Davey felt really free and he knew what he wanted to do. He went down to the old wooden pier behind the abandoned factories and waited for the Codfather. A little before noon, he eased up to the wobbly, old float and tied off. Then he proceeded to give the interior of the small vessel a thorough cleaning, bailed out the bilge and looked around making sure that everything was shipshape before stepping off the boat. Once on the float he turned and studied the vessel's condition one last time before making his way up the narrow wooden ramp.

"What are you looking for?" he asked the young man that was leaning on the post at the head of the ramp.

"Just looking to see if you needed any help," Davey replied. "I wanna learn about commercial fishing."

"Not right now, the summer run is on and all my gear is in the water and the lobstering is pretty good and it's something that I can handle by myself. But if you're around come mid-August, I'll be drying out my traps for worm season and setting out for conch. That's heavier work and I might be able to use a hand."

"I'll be around," Davey replied. Then he turned and walked away.

"Albie, can you teach me how to build lobster traps?" Davey had gone straight to Albie's house upon departing from his first face to face meeting with the Codfather.

"You got a job?" You got a lobster license? You need money

for all this stuff. Where are you gonna get bait?" Albie asked the young man.

"Yeah I've been working for Harry Johnson for the past few summers and I've got some money saved up," Davey announced.

"Well I don't know. I'll think about it. And I think that you'd better think about it really hard, because you'd better be really sincere in regards to such an effort before you go spending a lot of time and money and work on it."

The next morning, Davey headed out to go blue fishing at the Branford beacon. It's a large cross shaped reef that lies about two miles offshore. Where the four points of the reef meet stands a conical stone tower atop of which sits a large metal box housing a revolving flashing light. At a point where he was parallel to the Negro Head reef, a smaller straight and narrow reef about a mile offshore, he noticed Albie adrift in his boat. Davey steamed over to check on his old friend. Albie was just sitting on the low wooden bench seat that ran amidships from gunwale to gunwale just behind the center counsel. "What's wrong Albie?" Davey asked as he pulled alongside.

"I think she blew a piston," Albie replied. With that the two small boats became connected with a heavy nylon tow rope and Davey brought his fellow mariner back to the harbor and up into his slip safe and sound.

"Come over some night after supper and we'll build a lobster trap," Albie announced to Davey as he made his way up the pier. Davey showed up at Albie's that following evening and Albie taught him how to knit the nylon funnels for a lobster trap. That session was followed by another one in which they actually constructed a lobster trap. Then Albie showed Davey how to put together a gillnet. Then Davey went to the State Capital building and purchased a ten pot lobster license and a commercial finfish license to run his gillnet. Then he bought some raw material and made some gear and went fishing.

He set his gillnet about two-hundred yards off of Sunset beach in line with a half dozen others. First he dropped a hollow cinder block for an anchor in the water then threw out the trailer buoy. Then he paid out the net with the tide, the one-hundred feet of three inch monofilament mesh strung with small floats tied every six feet and weighted with lead core line to keep the net vertical, then released the other anchor and its trailer buoy.

The next morning, Davey woke early and headed out in the predawn light full of excitement and anticipation. This was his first experience in commercial fishing. Upon approaching his net, he noticed that some of the buoys were underwater and that others were bobbing up and down. He pulled the net into his boat along with a full bushel of menhaden along with a handful of small bluefish and a couple of nice weakfish.

At that point he reflected on a conversation with Albie some time before, where you gonna get your bait? Now he had bait, where you gonna get money for your gear? Well he and worked for it and earned it and built gear and presently he had fresh bait on board along with six brand-new oak lobster traps with an extra brick in them for the "first set," as Albie had instructed him, as the traps, being totally dry, could otherwise float on the surface, or the water between the surface and the bottom for an undetermined amount of time.

Davey headed for the Cow and Calf, a place where two rocks show below high tide and a fairly sizeable reef runs towards the west about a mile offshore. He set three traps close to the rocks and the other three a little ways off, out on the reef. The next morning he brought out four more traps, but before he set them out, he took note of the location in regards to the six traps that he had set on the previous morning. They looked to be in the same location. "Then wait three days," Albie told Davey.

It was tough for the excited lad to hold off; however three mornings later he set out to check his traps. And he had lobsters! He had shorts and keepers and he had conch and a few blackfish and starfish. There were spider crabs in some of the traps and jellyfish and seaweed and tiny clams and snails stuck in the mud that clung to the traps that weren't set on the reef. Davey couldn't believe the diversity of marine life that had made its way into his traps. He did well for most of the summer, coming up with a keeper in just about every other trap, and sometimes a keeper in every trap or even more. However, around the third week in August, the traps were coming up empty of lobsters and full of spider crabs.

One morning after hauling up a trap and placing it on the culling board that he had attached to the starboard gunwhale, Davey looked up and straight into the eyes of the Codfather. "Time to dry 'em out." Run's over and the worms are startin' to show up. See those white blotchy masses on the underside of that door? That's the toredo worm set. They start like that then they honeycomb through the wood and ruin your traps in a week. Put them on your boat and I'll show you where you can let them dry out."

Davey stacked five water logged, barnacle and sea moss laden traps in his boat and proceeded to follow the Codfather back to the harbor and upriver. At the head of the inner bay lay two large steel hulled barges rotting away on the mud flat. On one of them sat a large wooden pilot house with a flat roof. The Codfather tied up to the barge near the pilot house and motioned Davey to do the same. "Hand me those traps," the Codfather said to Davey with outstretched arms. Davey bucked the five heavy traps up to the Codfather, who gingerly disappeared with them around the far side of the pilot house, one at a time. "Come on up," he said, after the boat was unloaded.

Around the far side of the dilapidated structure was an old doorway. The Codfather had stacked the traps next to the entryway just outside. "You can store your traps here, the Codfather announced, but Albie has the rights to the inside. Meet me up at my dock if you want to go winkleing."

The Codfather was sitting on a couple of old lobster traps in the sparse shade of a stunted sumac tree, looking out at the river. In between his outstretched knees was a large spool of three-eighths black polypropylene buoy line. After pulling out a certain number of arm's lengths, he'd cut the line from the spool. "Forty to sixty-five feet of warp." Pull up a seat and a spool. Take thirteen arm's lengths then cut. I got eight brand-new winkle traps behind that stack of old lobster traps that need to be rigged. I figure forty in and forty out, and we'll rotate every week so that the worms don't get into 'em."

The next day they loaded twenty conch traps onto the Codfather's small wooden skiff and set them out in the sound. Davey didn't talk too much. He just listened and did what the Codfather told him to do. They baited the traps with a half of a horseshoe crab which was pushed down onto a twenty penny galvanized spike that was imbedded vertically in the middle of the inch and a half concrete slab poured in the bottom of the trap for ballast. Then a short section of garden hose with a small hole in the middle was pushed down on the nail to hold the bait in place.

It was a simple fishery with simple traps, and bait that was just picked off of the beaches during the week before and after the full moon on the flood tide in June. This is when these pre-historic creatures come up from the bottom of the sound and march up in the sand to the high tide mark to mate and dig a little spot, lay their eggs, cover them up then return back to the water. The Codfather had several large chest freezers packed full of horseshoe crabs that he had gathered in anticipation of this present event.

The traps themselves were just a square frame twenty-two inches wide made of an inch and one half oak, one on top and one on the bottom. Then twelve inch long oak lathe boards by an inch and a half wide were nailed to the frames an inch and a half apart. A small scrap of lathe was typically used as a spacing gauge. Then eight penny nails were applied to the inside corners of the top frame. Then the key to success was to take a double strand of thin nylon twine and run it around the nail heads that stuck out about an inch and a quarter from the inside of the frame, then tie it off as tight as you could. Then another nail was used to tighten the line by applying it between the two strands and winding it over and over again in what is known as a spanish windlass. And when it got piano string tight one would strike the nail into the frame. The simple beauty of this trap's design is that the conch crawls up and over the side, maneuvers itself over the taut twine and falls in. The twine, being set up far enough away from the frame acts as a barrier that pens the creatures in. Simple, yet extremely effective.

At first Davey didn't talk too much with the Codfather about anything besides their present fishing effort. The Codfather was content just being out on the water every day, his big sky blue eyes smiling at every moment as he absorbed his natural coexistence and the beauty and challenges in the world in which the two young men endeavored in. Davey also discovered a calm inner peace in their day to day voyages. No day out on the sound was quite the same and the Codfather adjusted their circuit in accordance with the wind and tides, making each trip a fluid, efficient and enjoyable experience.

As the two young men spent more time together, Davey began to learn more and more about the Codfather's past. He had grown up in a wealthy family in Branford. He had attended college in Virginia and graduated with a degree in business management. But he had always loved fishing and being out on the sound, so after college he moved to Montana and guided fly fishermen from shore and wooden rowboats on some of the midwest's most famous trout fishing waters. Even with those huge meaty hands and fingers he was an expert at fly-tying and a fly-rod was like a magic wand in his hands.

After four years of guiding he had become bored with the routine and moved back to Branford and a life out on the sound, and the rivers that flow into it and nourish it.

"Every season brings something different to fish for," he told Davey. That's the beauty of the sound and its tributaries. You can be fishing for lobsters when they're running in the spring and summer, and fishing for conch in the early fall, then back to lobsters up till the New Year, then clamming or oystering in the cold weather while the rest of the sound is asleep.

Over the next few years Davey and the Codfather would share many days together, on and off the water. They would fish for whatever they could catch enough of in the appropriate season, to sell mostly to the local crowd and make enough money to get by and sometimes a little more.

It seems as if everyone is born with a special talent or gift and Davey would come to learn that the Codfather's special gift was quite unique. He was able to harvest a rich bounty of whatever they set out after. It was almost as if the Codfather had a sixth sense, or that he could see the bottom of the sound or river or estuary that they were fishing. Or maybe a vision came to him in his sleep. Whatever it was it amazed and fascinated Davey and little by little the Codfather would teach his young friend the secrets of making a living on the sound.

Chapter 6
Settin In

The Codfather bought a bigger boat that following spring. He and Davey had fished a little over a hundred lobster traps the previous fall hauling them out the week after Christmas. "If it's gonna' keep being the two of us, we need to fish more gear. This oughta do," he announced as he led Davey down the ramp to check out the new craft.

Davey was impressed and excited when he boarded the Codfather's new fishing vessel. She was a twenty-three foot Nova Scotia hull, an open skiff with a center console, and a small enclosed storage cabin up forward. She was planked with white pine over oak ribs with a nice wide gunwale and plenty of open deck space. She had a davit on the starboard side parallel to the center of the consol which housed a gasoline powered eight horsepower hauling motor.

"I think that we could do a lot more of everything with this rig," the Codfather announced proudly as he stepped up to the helm and grasped the wheel tightly with his two baseball glove sized hands. So that spring they set out one hundred and sixty lobster traps, and the Codfather had his gillnets which they set for their bait. And he purchased an otter trawl which is a net that one tows from the boat and can be set at different depths depending on what one is fishing for. The nylon meshed net tapered from thirty-three feet wide by three feet high on either side, down to twenty-two feet at the head of the cod end, the part of the net that tapered off into a narrow funnel which contained the catch.

It seemed to Davey that the Codfather had high expectations for the upcoming season as well as did Davey. However, as in many of life's diversified and uncontrollable experiences, the two young men were in for an unexpected drought in regards to what they were looking to harvest. And that's sometimes the way it goes. The nets came up empty, and the trawl only produced trash fish. And even with that as bait, the spring lobster run never materialized.

"Can't ever count on a good spring," the Codfather announced to Davey with no negative tone to his voice. We're fishing for the native population of lobsters in the sound and their pattern and abundance is very unpredictable. They could be feeding on barnacles on the reefs, or red crabs out on the mud, but if they got enough, they won't pot up until after they shed. And the finfish have been hit pretty hard by the mid-sound trawlers. That's why the gillnets aren't producing. And those large bottom draggers that we've been seeing all about are really putting a hurting on our efforts with the otter trawl. "It's time to make a move," the Codfather announced to his eager friend. "We're goin' shad fishin'."

The Codfather seemed to have an inexhaustible amount of funds in regards to his fishing efforts as long as he showed strong direction and confidence. So they went to Wilcox Marine Supplies, in Stonington, and brought everything that they needed to mobilize and execute for the Codfather's latest adventure. They put together a really long gillnet, six-hundred feet, more or less. It was constructed of five and one-quarter inch nylon mesh with break strength of twenty-seven pounds. They strung small buoys every six feet on the top and she was weighted down with three-eighths lead core line. Then they built two wooden lantern boxes which would float kerosene lamps.

Davey was totally unfamiliar with this particular fishery, and he was totally looking forward to the experience.

The Connecticut river originates from its connection with Long Island sound some three hundred miles almost due north, in Canada, in the northern foothills of the White Mountains. A series of lakes and dams harvest the pristine waters of an unknown number of mountain streams and run-offs of various size and strength. Below the final dam, the mighty river emerges in earnest, blossoming into a constant steady flow. From that conception, it grows stronger and wider on its deliberate, unending task of gathering life and sharing life on its journey southward and finally into the sound.

Even though the Connecticut has a lengthy history of industrial development along its shores and had been heavily polluted by man's efforts to progress, it's starting to regress back into its wild natural state, now that people seem to have an awareness of the many benefits that come from that condition, which was present for the Native Americans who lived in close proximity to its banks, and seasonally harvested its bounty, as well as the first white settlements that did likewise.

So there they were, with a fourteen foot wooden scow atop a rusty old trailer which was attached to the Cod father's rusty old green Ford pickup at the state launching ramp at Hale's Landing in Rocky Hill, ready to go fishing.

The Codfather carefully loaded up the small scow, marking the location of each item, and making sure that Davey knew where everything should be stowed. "Its dusk 'till dawn," he told Davey. "We ain't gotta lot of room and we gotta keep things simple. You'll see why by the end of the night." Then when it was their turn, they launched the small, cluttered but organized craft then slowly made their way downstream, past the paved ramp and wooden pier and down to a long straight stretch of low willows overhanging the river bank. The Codfather proceeded to pull up right underneath the overhanging branches and tie the boat off.

A half dozen other small wooden craft were spaced out down river, tethered in similar fashion, waiting their turn to put in.

"Albie showed me this whole routine," the Codfather said to Davey, breaking the silence. "You know Albie?" Davey asked, standing up from the center wooden seat. "I've known Albie for a long time," the Codfather proudly announced. Davey regained his seat amid ships. "He's taught me a lot about the water and has given me a lot of inspiration about life in general. Watch what's happening now. Watch that lantern in the boat across the river, drifting towards that blinking green light down in that dark corner. See that tall oak on the darkening horizon behind the boat and just down river. When that boat aligns with that tree, he'll turn out that light, signaling time for the next person to set in."

That's the halfway point of the first reach. It's common courtesy. It's like being able to justify your own action, and be accountable for your own actions. Everyone was born with a conscience. Everyone who is present, sharing in this experience, deserves an equal chance. "Space the nets equally and you'll sleep good at night", that's the way Albie taught me. So the two young men waited their turn to set the net in. It was a clear, cool mid-April evening, and the river was calm but running strong and steady. The waiting period was a great time for them to get tuned in with their natural surroundings.

The river is quite wide at this point in its journey, probably the better part of a half mile. And the first reach was well over a mile long, the river running straight and true, of which one could study its entire length, all the way down to a corner, which on the eastern bank stood a low stone tower atop of which is a green flashing light. From the staging point under the willows, both banks were totally uninhabited throughout this stretch, without a trace of mankind, probably due to the fact that inland from the water's edge the earth is flat and swampy. So far man has made no attempt at civilizing or industrializing this part of the river. Thick stands of alder and willows and red maple grow profusely along its banks, broken up in spots by light green patches of eelgrass, dancing ever so gently in the quickly darkening sky.

And there were lots of big birds around; birds of prey, fishing birds. Davey always had a strong connection with fishing birds. You could learn a lot from them, he came to think, after noting their behavior throughout the years. First of all, when they're around, he knew that the fish would be around. And he learned that different fishing birds fish for different fish. The herons and egrets primarily fish in the marshes or right along the shore, wading in the shallows, constantly focusing their attention below the surface of the water directly in front of them, searching and waiting for the opportunity to strike at small baitfish with their long, spear-like beaks. In the sky above the river there could be seen osprey and occasionally bald eagles or even a golden eagle. These big birds fished for big fish, and when one of them would flutter for sometimes five or ten seconds or so, then launch itself down below the river's surface, and reappear, sometimes with a fish thrashing in its talons, it meant to Davey that a successful trip was at hand. And they were all present on that first memorable evening on the river. It's amazing, Davey thought to himself, how great an example of the delicate balance of nature.

Human technology nearly wiped out the big birds of prey along the length of the Connecticut, as well as many other rivers in the northeast. Without thinking of the future, and with no consideration regarding the effects that would evolve by their actions, people nearly wiped out the big birds of prey by introducing untested pesticides into a very delicate and vulnerable ecosystem. Fortunately when left alone, nature has an awesome tenacious primordial instinct to survive and proliferate. The big birds were back, and it was a beautiful, honorable sight to experience. Then it was their turn to set in. "Gonna be a good night," the Codfather said softly.

The Codfather then proceeded to pull out a short ways into the river and then swing their strength in such a manner in which the well equipped, sturdy little wooden craft lied perpendicular to the river's current, its stern facing the opposite bank. "Full moon tonight, lots of energy, I can almost see the shad swimming underneath the boat. They're swimmin' hard, the river runs from the north and that full moon is just a pullin them right up. Take that buttoned jacket off now boy, as every mesh of that net will find its way behind them buttons and we'll have a mess on our hands. Can't you see that everything on this ship is as smooth as a baby's ass? Regardless of what you're fishing for boy, everything's gotta be right. Now set in that lantern box and pay out that net and keep it taut."

Davey placed the wooden lantern box and its dull yellow glow into the river. Then the Codfather proceeded to back the small vessel across the river, heading just enough downstream to compensate for the current and keep the net straight. When the net was fully paid out the Codfather shut the motor off, and standing erect and proud, began to row. "Gotta pull hard to keep her taut," he instructed Davey, "You'll learn."

Then with his round face and shining blue eyes and the crazy curly long thick hair that surrounded his face in the dim glow of the lantern on the bow, the Codfather began to ramble on. "I'm thinkin' that the moon affects lots of things in nature Davey. You just pay attention and maybe you'll come to the same conclusion. Like when the tide is a running real hard, that energy seems to spark a primitive, subconscious inner strength within everything in the water. And it seems like even the weather is affected by the moon. Mark it well sailor, seems to me that the most powerful storms here in the northeast come with the moon tide, be it new or full. Seems to me these storms get drawn into the warm gulf stream waters just off the coast then up, by the extra unseen magnetic connection between the moon and the pole. And it seems that with a moon tide, when the tide changes, the wind usually shifts direction, and there's a good chance that she'll come on strong. Just a few things to think about Davey, maybe it'll help you out sometime."

The Codfather proceeded to row, pulling methodically on the long wooden oars. And that is how they fished for shad. The lantern box was set in the fast current side of the river and the net was paid across, and they had to row all night in order to keep the net taut and at right angles to the riverbank. There were two "change overs." When the lantern began to slow down and their boat got ahead of the dim light, the Codfather would start up the motor, fasten their end of the net to a cleat under the bow, back the boat up till the net was taut, then unfasten the line and tie the other lantern box to it and drop it in the river. Then they would slowly proceed upriver above the net, and across, and pick up the other lantern box, douse the light, then proceed. Thus they kept the net fishing on their journey down river in the dark, in the most productive manner.

About four miles downstream from their original starting point, lies a fairly long, narrow island parallel to the flow, right in the middle of the river. When the dark shadow of trees on the island broke the unbounded vista of stars and moon to the south, the Codfather turned on the pole light, which was a simple portable one hundred watt light attached to a two by four that slid and stood vertically into a bracket attached to the starboard side of the small center consol.

With the light illuminating a concentrated, intimate work area the Codfather maneuvered the small circle of perception first around the boat, making sure that everything was in order then focused it onto the long row of small white football shaped buoys of the top water that faded quickly into the darkness beyond. "We got fish," the Codfather announced quietly. "See them buoys dancing and bobbing and being pulled under? We got fish. Then the two young men began the long tedious task of hauling in the net. The Codfather worked the buoy line and Davey worked the lead line; one with the left hand and one with the right and with opposite hands reaching into the middle, grabbing the mesh and stacking it neatly into the box.

Soon the first fish appeared and it was a shad, its long bright silvery white large scaled body struggled in the grip of the net. The Codfather grabbed it up, then deftly untangled the squirming creature and threw it into a wooden fish box that lay just ahead of the consol. The net was alive with fish. Not only the very marketable american shad which is a large member of the herring family, its flesh and roe being a unique seasonal and regional delicacy, there were many other species of fish struggling within the confines of the mesh. There were carp, which were thrown into a separate fish box for lobster bait, and catfish and pike and occasionally an atlantic sturgeon would come up, like some prehistoric remnant of the deep.

When the net and lantern box were back in the boat, the Codfather maneuvered the light around the boat again, making sure that everything was in order, and then he focused its brightness onto their catch. One fish box was nearly full with shad. Another box held a half dozen large, fat carp, and an equal amount of two to four pound catfish.

Not bad for the first drift," the Codfather announced. Davey just sat quietly on the gunwale, looking at the fish, which were still flopping and gasping for breath. Then the Codfather turned off the pole light and everything went black. "Takes a minute for your eyes to get adjusted to the dark," he said, turning his attention towards the southwestern horizon, where the moon's shadow of the tree line was cast onto the silent flowing river. They just drifted for a bit, towards the darkness of the island that loomed closer and closer in the middle of the river, and slowly, everything around them came into perspective.

Looking back up river, channel lights were blinking from fixed positions on the banks, and lanterns were glowing and drifting in the current marking the progress of other nets fishing their way down river. But other than that it was just the two young fishermen and their natural environment. The moon seemed to be flowing downstream, past the treetops, and all of the heavenly bodies seemed to be moving accordingly, but in reality it was their small craft that was connected with the river's flow.

The engine came to life and the Codfather slowly came about, slowly idling up river. "What's next," Davey asked. He was presently feeling a little apprehensive in regards to their safe return to the landing, in a small, fairly laiden boat, on a big, dark primitive river. The Codfather let out a long deep hearty chuckle and then announced to Davey, "Let's go back and do it again." With that he proceeded to firmly push the throttle lever to the full position, and steam upriver in the dim light provided by the moon and stars. "Hold on boy, this is the fun part," he advised Davey as the boat rapidly gained speed.

Davey sat on the deck, his back up against the fish boxes and his legs bent up with his feet on the edge of the net box. At first he was downright scared, feeling he had no control of his immediate destiny. The Codfather sensed the young man's apprehension. "Don't worry boy," he said loud enough to be heard over the methodical hum of the engine. "I've done this a hundred times before." Davey relaxed and just accepted the fact that his present fate was in the hands of the Codfather, focusing his attention on his intensely squinting eyes and tightly smiling lips. On their way upriver the Codfather hugged the eastern bank giving a wide berth to the other fishermen, whose presence was only detected by the dim, flickering light of their lantern making its way down river. Then after about twenty minutes of dodging branches and following the dim riverbank they were back to the landing, and crossed the river and took their place in line. And when it was their turn, they set the net again. And they got three drifts in that night before the first light of false dawn greeted them halfway back up to the willows.

Then when they could see again, in the natural light of the new day, a feeling of relief and accomplishment overcame Davey. "Now look all around you, and try to mark everything well, that's how you learn the reach. See the tree line on the far bank and were it ends and the marsh grass takes over the shoreline, well that's the second changeover. And see the blinking light up ahead of us and above where the river runs straight north to south, well that's called the cold hole, you'll see why it's called that sometime, that's the first changeover." The Codfather then let out a deep hearty laugh as he proceeded to inspect their catch.

"We got two-hundred-and-forty pounds of shad there boy, at least, plus some bait for the lobster gear, and some fish to have a little fun with when we get back to the landing." When they arrived at the ramp, a small varied racial crowd of men were milling around in the parking lot. There was also a large rack bodied pick-up truck parked just above the river's edge with its tailgate open. There was a round scale mounted above a flat wooden platform set up above the open gate. The Codfather and Davey unloaded the four boxes of shad from the boat and carried them up to the back of the pick-up.

"How much today Sonny?" The Codfather directed his question to a short, wiry, middle aged man who was standing, arms folded across his chest, at the back of the truck next to the scale. The man looked down and studied their catch. Then, seconds later he quickly straightened up, drew himself face to face with the Codfather and announced in a quick raspy voice, "Ninety cents a pound for the roe fish (egg bearing females) and fifty cents for the buckies." The Codfather again let out one of his familiar deep hearty laughs. He then bent down, grabbed up a large female shad and aiming its posterior directly in the man's face, squeezed firmly on the fish's belly. A couple seconds later he dropped the fish back into the box and firmly announced, "When that row comes a' squirtin' out and hits you in the eye, then you can ask me for ninety cents a pound. Let's go Davey, put the shad in my pick-up." As they started walking away with the first box, the man dashed in front of them and with his hands flailing in the air, he agreed to raise the price. "Alright Codfather, one-twenty and sixty, and that's as high as I'll go."

"That's still dirt cheap, but I guess it's still better than runnin' into the city," the Codfather replied, followed by another hearty laugh.

So they sold their shad to Sonny, two-hundred and twenty pounds of roe fish and forty-two pounds of buckies. And the man gave the Codfather a piece of paper with the date, pounds, and price, which after a quick inspection, he crumpled it up and stuffed it into his pocket. And like that, the shad were gone. "Now let's make a little spending money," the Codfather said to his friend as he walked back to the little scow. They were followed by the small group of on-lookers who were patiently waiting their turn to purchase some fresh fish.

"Come on Davey; help me get this box onto the culling board." They set the box on the middle of the culling board and the Codfather proceeded to achieve a relaxed position on the end of the oak board, towards the bow. There was no scale, no fixed price per pound and no bartering. The people formed a small line and approached one at a time, with plastic bags in hand. "That big catfish?" asked the first customer. "Three dollars," answered the Codfather, while producing a small coffee can from the storage shelf inside the council. "Any shad?" asked the next person. The Codfather looked over and noted that the man who had just bought the shad was just pulling out of the parking lot. Then he reached to the bottom of the fishbox and pulled out two buckey shad. "He ain't gettin 'em all," he said, slapping the brace of fish on top of the pile. "Two dollars each, he firmly announced. And when the box was empty and the crowd gone, all that was left were the two young men with a box of carp for lobster bait, a piece of paper with some numbers on it to be tallied up with the others at the end of the week for payment on the shad, a little spending money, and the broad, flowing river flowing silently at their feet.

"Get some sleep," the Codfather said to his exhausted friend as he pulled into Davey's driveway. "That was an easy night, tomorrow when we get back, we gotta go pull the lobster traps. See ya at five."

And so they fished. One night on the river after the first drift, the Codfather beached the small scow on a gravely little spit of sand at the base of the flashing channel marker which he called the "Cold Hole," on their way back up to the landing. A slight northerly breeze had made up, sending a shiver down Davey's already damp spine. "Whatta we doin' here?" Davey asked the Codfather. He was anxious to get back on the oars, in order to keep himself warm.

"Just stayin' in touch with some of my friends," he answered quietly, as he hunkered up onto the culling board, crossing one leg over the other and turning his heavily bearded face into the wind.

Davey assumed his usual position when he wasn't rowing or working the net, sitting facing the bow with his back up against the counsel, knees bent and feet up on the edge of the fish box. He was tired and the cool evening breeze felt refreshing on his face. He closed his eyes and just thought about where he was and this very special thing that he was presently part of. He thought back to the words that Albie had spoken to him. "You like fishing because it's free." And Davey thought to himself, yeah, Albie was right. I love fishing because it's free. I'm free. I'm a free spirit. We're in this simple little boat and we made some simple fishing equipment, and we're out here on this big, wild river, catchin' fish and makin' money and completely tuned into and part of our natural surroundings.

Just then as he dozed off while listening to the branches in the blackness above the dim shoreline, he was startled to full consciousness by a scratchy thump-thump of small feet of the bow, not six feet from his present location. And in a dreamlike state, Davey leaned up from his resting position and peered directly into two sets of small yellow eyes with wide black stripes springing from either side. Two little bandits, Davey thought to himself as he waited motionless to see what would happen next. The Codfather coaxed the two raccoons forward. "Come on guys, come and get your share, its O.K." They slowly eased their way over the smooth, flat bow plank and quickly grabbed up the two small bucky shad that the Codfather had been holding for them with outstretched arms. The two adolescent raccoons hesitated for a moment, turning back at the tip of the bow and looking at the Codfather as if to say thanks. Then they pushed the fish off and quickly followed into the darkness.

"Usually, raccoons will only eat what they kill Davey, but I've been sharin' my catch with these critters and their parents and grandparents for years. They trust me, and they know that I'm here to live on this earth in peaceful harmony with all living creatures. Yeah I kill a lot of fish, we kill a lot of fish, but when you give to nature, nature will give back to you. You can't just take all the time," the Codfather spoke softly to his astounded friend. "It becomes a balance in your life. You'll find that if you take too much and never give anything back in return, chances are you'll be struggling most of the time. Give and take and you will be rewarded in many, many ways. And an inner peace will come over you, knowing that you're in balance with nature and that nature accepts you and welcomes your presence with open arms. Don't fight it, when the weather is bad, or you question why, when you work so hard and think that everything is perfect and the nets or traps come up nearly empty just go with the flow, and enjoy the experience, and always find a way to share the bounty, no matter how big or how small it may be," the Codfather had sensed that Davey was only focused on the job at hand, and trying to work as hard as he could, and to do the best that he could, However, he wanted Davey to totally observe the whole experience.

After that night, Davey began to relax, and appreciate his natural surroundings. It was coming in to the end of April, the conclusion of the second week of the season. Davey saw and heard and very much appreciated the many sights and sounds of spring ushering in renewed life and color all around him.

When the sun had set and twilight had fallen upon them, Davey and the Codfather waited their turn to set out. They were third in line, with three more boats waiting behind them. Cauldy was usually there first, being a native to these parts and the only other full-time fisherman on the river. Unlike Davey and the Codfather however, he only fished the river. The other guys were part-timers, having other "real jobs" and just made a drift or two to earn some extra cash. As they waited their turn to set in, the river's steady powerful flow slowly faded into darkness. And as it did so, the peepers began to awaken, small unseen tree frogs that thrive in the lowlands. At first there could be heard a sporadic peep, coming from different locations along the shoreline, and with various stages of volume. However not long after full darkness had set in, their tune became a constant loud, high pitched whistle that reverberated along the entire shoreline.

Then it was their turn and they set the net and rowed, watching the lantern on its voyage, a slave to the currents of the river. The peepers methodical hum, and the sound of the oars dipping into the river then drawing back out into the air, and a fish flapping, caught in the net near the surface close to the buoy line and struggling vainly for its freedom, guided them through the long dark night. And when the night sky was clear, they passed the time noting the various constellations that could be seen from their location. The Codfather knew many of them, and shared his knowledge in regards to each one, and other prominent stars, and how they moved in space and time, and that movement and relationship seems like it was something one could count on for quite some time. And when morning broke, usually on their way back up-river after their third drift, they both felt more confident and fuller and wiser from their experience.

One morning with no wind, which was usually the case, a thick low ground fog that had formed in the adjacent lowland, slowly crept out into the main body of the river. Sometimes the building mass on one bank would intertwine with the one materializing from the other, and would briefly dance together and become one before being drawn up into one unified mass and hover above the river's surface. At times, the two opposite phonemes would approach each other, both moving towards mid-river, then hesitate at any unmeasured distance apart, then seemingly after acknowledging one another, would rise up on an indistinguishable breeze and disappear into the ever brightening morning sky.

Davey resolved in the opening of spring along the riverbank. The low marsh grass was achieving a darker green shiny hue day by day. And he observed the deep sodden banks, which fell off into the river at the base of the grass become a darker brown, being enriched by a multitude of unseen life, which flowed up into the marshes with the flood tide and were drawn back into the river from the insatiable earth on the outgoing.

The swamp maples were in bloom along both shores; their thick clusters of red buds signaled the beginning of spring opening in the unbroken canopy of forest beyond the low marshlands. And that reflection in the river's calmness in the first light of dawn presented a surrealistic feeling that one was not on the surface of the water, nor in the sky, but somewhere in between. And there were plenty of different species of birds arriving to share their presence, and to prosper in the richness of spring on the river. The unmistakable chatter of kingfishers was a common evening and morning sound, although this elusive medium-sized blue-grey bird with crested head and white and grey markings on its upper chest was hardly ever spotted. Flying low below the tree line, these remarkable fishermen would come to an abrupt halt upon spotting a potential meal with their keen eyes, then helicopter high above the river formulating a plan of attack, then swiftly rocket down, disappearing momentarily beneath the surface of the water and usually reappearing with a squirming shiny meal. There were ospreys as well and they fished in the same manner only for larger fish. And occasionally a bald or golden eagle would be sighted. And there were the fishermen of birds that fished the riverbanks. And there were great blue herons, green herons, white herons, and snowy egrets, to name a few, which patiently waded the shoreline in search of their small bait-fish prey.

And the sights and sounds of a varied multitude of songbirds filled the ever ripening meadows and adjacent woodlands. There were red-winged blackbirds, and bluebirds and finches and robins to name a few. And their songs and their colorful presence filled the sky above the river and its adjacent woodlands in the day. And in the predawn mist, as the shadows chasing away the dark-ness melted vagueness into familiar forms, they would slowly begin their songs again, gaining in volume, with the confidence that a new day was truly upon them.

And so that's how it was in the spring of Davey's eighteenth year. It was shad fishing all night on the Connecticut river, lob-stering out on the sound, working hard and sleeping a little, em-bracing each past experience and looking forward to the next one.

The Codfather and Davey came to be a well-matched crew, bonded together both in their tasks and their experiences as well as their mutual love, respect and thankfulness in regards to just doing it. It was hard work; it seemed as if anything taken for a price from Mother Nature never came easy. The young men had to deal with many different and sometimes unexpected obstacles. With springtime on the wane, the river had become noticeably lower due to the lack of rain for several weeks. It was common for a net to get hung up on one submerged object or another on its slow meander down river. This threw the fishermen out of rhythm, having to pull the net into the object of interference, free it up, and then pay it back out again. And as the evenings grew warmer, the task became more physically demanding. The Cod-father, after hanging the net for the first time, took immediate action. They pulled the net to the snag, freed it and pulled the remainder into the boat and steamed to the landing. Under the lights of the two lanterns and the pole light, he and Davey proceeded to wind up four feet of the lead lines on the entire net and tie if off onto itself. "Not as much mesh, not as many fish, but hopefully no more hangs," the Codfather announced to Davey upon completing the arduous task and setting the net out once again.

Then one night, the dry conditions and low water almost cost them their lives. It was a still dark moonless night. The Codfather had executed two flawless drifts and they already had a descent catch on board.

The lantern box was just beginning to slow down on the far side of the river, along the long low stretch of unseen eelgrass that lined the bank. The Codfather looked up to the south as he pulled hard on the oars, peering hard into the darkness, looking for a sign that they were drawing close to the island at the end of the last reach. Davey was watching the distant glow in the lantern box when suddenly it started swinging toward the center of the channel.

"We're hung up," Davey announced calmly. He figured that this being near the end of the last reach on their final drift of the night, that they would pull the net, free it from the snag and call it quits. The Codfather took the oars from the oarlocks and placed them on the deck, just inside either gunwale. Then he turned around facing the council and reached for the pole light switch. Then he straightened up tall, and took a deep breath then froze momentarily, peering downstream wide eyed as if in some sort of trance. Davey focused his attention downriver in the direction of the Codfather's bewilderment. What he saw made the adrenaline flowing through his veins elevate his consciousness into an intense state of awareness.

"Tow boat," the Codfather said. He didn't panic, but he was still frozen in a state of disbelief, not yet quite sure of what to do. Davey saw lights, lots of lights, lots of different colored brightly flowing lights. There were two rows of white lights running horizontally about forty feet apart from one another and about fifteen feet above their line of vision. Then above them were green and red and white lights reaching high into the starry night. And these silent lights were not too far away, having just cleared the shadow of the island, and were coming toward them like one giant silently moving Christmas tree.

The Codfather, upon making his decision, sprang quickly into action. He turned on the pole light and fired up the motor. "He ain't far and he sees us now with the pole light on and he'll take it out of gear, but only for so long. Pull like hell and we'll cut it clean at the hang and he might pass clear of the other half if we can back off in time and give a wide enough berth. And if we don't, he'll steer to port and we'll lose the other half in those giant propellers of his."

"You think we have time?" Davey asked in a soft tone. He was totally sure that the Codfather would make the right decision, however he wanted to make sure that he gave it enough thought.

"Pull like hell," the Codfather replied, "We can do it, I don't wanna lose this whole net, let alone the fish that are in it.

Leaving the motor running they hauled the heavily fish laden net into the boat. With the net being hung up on the bottom however, at some point in the middle of the channel, they had to pull the boat to the hang, instead of pulling the net to the boat. It seemed like it took forever to pull two outstretched arms lengths of net and fish aboard. Meanwhile those lights on that big, silent Christmas tree were getting closer and brighter.

As they neared mid-river the Codfather straightened up, and took a moment to consider thier present situation. "He's out of gear but he can't stay that way for long, otherwise the current will turn him sideways, and he won't let that happen. He's slowing down but with all that oil in that barge that he's towing his momentum ain't gonna slow down for a spell. We're almost across the channel, just another hundred feet and we'll be clear, pull like hell."

So they pulled for all that they were worth and finally a big waterlogged branch emerged from the blackness and into their small circle of light. The Codfather produced a gleaming razor sharp knife from a sheath attached to the side of the council, grabbed up all the mesh from the buoy line to the lead line and with four long smooth strokes of his arm he cut the net through, just ahead of the hang and set them free to the river's current.

As the stern swung downriver, Davey looked to starboard. Instantly his senses changed their focus as he heard the deep steady low hum of the powerful diesels. Looking skyward, the lights were right there, right upon them. Then the dull white wash of the barge was right alongside them in their little field of vision. Then a wall of black steel, heavily encrusted with a jagged looking layer of dull white barnacles was all that could be seen. Their little scow raked alongside the barge momentarily but the Codfather slowly eased them away from the giant hulking mass. The Codfather shut the motor off and they silently drifted downriver, regaining their composure, the lights and the rumble of the towboat slowly faded into the blackness. The lantern in the box attached to the other half of the net was barely a flicker of light far downriver on the east side of the island. The Codfather eased downriver in unfamiliar waters and they caught up to it and pulled it into the boat. Amazingly enough, the towboat had missed it completely. Then they slowly steamed upstream, back to the landing, in the first shadows of the new day.

Presently it came to be mid June, and the two young men were at the physical and mental limits of their capabilities. Their hands were full of cuts from the mesh and fish gillplates which were razor sharp and cut deep and clean if one wasn't paying the utmost attention when handling the shad. And it seemed that as they became more and more worn down by their perseverant efforts of fishing all night on the river and tending to the sixty lobster traps every third day that they had fishing for them out on the sound, their minds lost the keen focus needed to avoid physical injury.

One evening, while waiting their turn under the willows to set in for their first drift, the Codfather produced a long clear tube with a small string attached to a round molded eye in the top. Whistling lightly under his breath, he turned his back to Davey and lowered the thermometer into the river. A minute later he quickly pulled it out of the water and held it right in front of his squinting eyes. Then he took a deep breath and turned around and looking like he had been relieved of some great burden, flipped over an empty fish box and fairly collapsed onto it in a sitting position.

"It's over, it's over boy, it's over," he announced to his faithful friend.

"How can you say that, we've been catchin" good, real good for the past couple weeks. Watta you getting' tired, you wanna give up?" Davey answered in a state of denial and disbelief.

"See this, see the red line in this tube, what's it read boy, you tell me."

"Sixty degrees," Davey replied after studying the thermometer. "Looks like the water temperature is sixty degrees."

"Mark that number well boy, and mark it well how things change in the sound and its tributaries and estuaries when the water temperature hits sixty degrees. It's like a magic number of sorts for a multitude of changes."

It was like someone had waved a magic wand down upon the river on that warm memorable clear mid June evening under a big, bright yellow full moon. They caught a lot of shad on their first drift, but only a handful that had a belly full of roe.

"Notice how most of the fish are hung up on the north side of the net boy. They're spawned out and are heading back to sea."

After one drift, the Codfather didn't return to their spot in line under the willow but pulled up to the ramp and the landing, tying up to a moss covered piling. "Let's go get some rest, we both deserve it," he said to Davey as he dragged his scaly rubber coated body up the dark pavement and collapsed in the front seat of the pick-up.

When morning came, the man who had bought their shad all spring long was standing outside the Codfather's window. "It's over huh?" he said, with his head staring down at the black pavement of the parking lot.

"Yes, another season, another handful of memories, the end of one experience yet the beginning of another," the Codfather replied.

"What have you got?" the man inquired in regards to their catch. "One box, maybe six roe fish. The rest are buckies or all spawned out then heading for God only knows where."

"Codfather you again brouht me more fish than any of the other boats this season, so as a reward and a small token of my sincere gratitude, I'll give you forty cents a pound for that trash."

"Thanks for your very generous offer my dear friend, however I feel like dining on shad tonight and we're getting low on lobster bait. See you in the spring Sonny, come on Davey let's go home." Davey learned a lot that spring, not only about the water and about fishing, but he thought that the best and most important lesson that he had learned from the Codfather was to never distance one's self from someone with less experience. The Codfather had never made Davey feel that he was less than himself, but only strived to make Davey a better, more knowledgeable fisherman.

Chapter 7

A Broken Line

After the close of the shad fishing season, Davey and the Codfather's life became much simpler. They focused their fishing efforts entirely on lobstering and catching their own bait for their traps. The long drive up to Rocky Hill and the long nights on the Connecticut river, and the even longer, almost surrealistic ride back to Branford each morning, were now only an interwoven group of memories.

The Codfather, as always, fished with great focus and intensity. Now the summer shedder run was upon them, and the Codfather stressed the importance to Davey, not in words, but with action, to keep fresh bait in the traps. He also kept a keen eye out for any slight irregularity with each trap that was handled onto the culling board. A lathe could be warped just enough for a keeper to escape. A brick could be loose, and crush the lobsters on their vertical ascent from the bottom. A mesh in one of the funnels could be frayed or broken, allowing a keeper to escape. No trap went back into the water with fresh bait without being "fishable" as the Codfather called it.

Their catch was good, real good, from mid June through mid August. They were fishing roughly two hundred traps, pulling roughly one third of them each day, basically fishing three day sets and they were accruing at least two bushels of lobsters a day, more or less. Then, come mid August, many "green eggers," egg bearing females with a fresh crop of eggs exposed under their tails, which were not allowed to be harvested in Long Island sound, began to show up in the traps, and the little blotchy white clusters of the toredo worm larvae were beginning to appear on the wooden traps.

"Time to go for conch," the Codfather announced. So they set in to the arduous task of bringing in their two hundred heavy, water logged moss and barnacle covered lobster traps. The Codfather seemed as if he couldn't get enough time in on the water. Conch fishing wasn't enough to fill his insatiable appetite for fishing for something, so he told Davey that they were going oystering as well, to fill in the down time. "Conch move slow so we don't need to be out there every day. Besides, it ain't a lot of money, but it keeps us in touch with the sound," So the Codfather put the shad scow back into action.

Oystering was yet another very simple fishery. They harvested oysters from the bottom of the Branford river and along its grassy banks, as well as the Farm river in East Haven and the mighty Housatonic in Stratford. Due to state regulations, a hand-pulled dredge was the most sophisticated means of harvest on state grounds. So they employed their little three foot dredge with its long row of two inch metal teeth and its chain and nylon basket just upstream from the mouths of these rivers in the brackish water where the oysters thrive. And thrive they did. Again the Codfather displayed an almost magical sense as to the location of the richest oyster beds at the bottom of these waters.

It was hard work. The dredge in itself was heavy even without any oysters. The frame of the dredge was heavy steel. There was a v-shaped bar with a closed ring on the top to which a shackle was secured. The tow line was fastened to the shackle. The bottom of each side of the v was bent down on an angle and attached to this was a heavy flat steel plate which the teeth were welded to. On the back of the ground plate was a square section of steel rings as wide as the plate and about two feet long. The rings formed the bottom of the basket, being heavy and durable. The top part of the basket was constructed of heavy hand-knitted nylon mesh which was fastened to the perimeter of the steel rings, then onto the bend in the main dredge bar. The top of the basket being hand woven, gave the fisherman the capability to adjust the size of the basket by simply removing that part of the dredge and reattaching a larger or smaller section of mesh. Typically the Codfather and Davey fished with a rig that could hold about a bushel and a half of oysters when full. A full dredge probably weighed close to one hundred and fifty pounds!

Davey soon came to realize that the Codfather knew about all of these different fisheries, and how to be successful at them, through experience. He carefully observed everything that the Codfather did and stored it in his memory. The way that the Codfather handled that little scow boat in regards to its employment in catching oysters was truly outstanding to behold. He'd get on his range; although he never told Davey exactly what it was, then simply give Davey a little nod of his head. Davey would then heave the dredge overboard, trying to land it flat on the river's surface. Then the predetermined amount of line would be laid out (usually about six times the depth of the water) then when all the slack was taken up to the cleat on the starboard mid-ship the little boat would come to a lurching halt. And if one wasn't paying attention, he could easily be tossed to the deck or even overboard by this abrupt jolt. Then the Codfather would throttle up, and achieve the speed of a slow walk, always towing upriver into the current.

"Hold the line Davey and tell me what you feel." Davey would lean over the gunwale, grab the heavy braided nylon tow line in his hand and pull back slightly. When they were over oysters, he could feel the dredge rattling them up and into the basket. "You're on 'em," Davey would reply. When they were "on 'em," which was more often than not, the Codfather would tow the dredge for about another hundred yards. Then the Codfather would turn the boat broadside to the current and they would simply drift downstream to the dredge with Davey taking up the slack as they went. There was one tricky part to their system. This was in the timing of the two young men pulling hard and fast together to get the dredge up off of the bottom and up alongside the gunwale before the boat drifted past it.

Every river was a unique experience, and every drift was a little different than the previous one. However one thing that didn't change was the fact that they always had a boat full of oysters on their way back to the dock. It was mid fall, a beautiful time of year to be on the water. Typically the day would pass by with only the encounter of a few hardy sport-fishermen coming and going, all bundled up in their colorful oilskins. And it was a peaceful time of year, filled with quiet moments of reflections, as well as somber moments of anticipation regarding the cold months that lay ahead. The swamp maples turned a fiery crimson red, and Davey thought back to springtime and shad fishing on the Connecticut. He recalled the scattered dense stands budding deep red in the early spring, "First to bud, first to turn," he thought to himself. And he marked the other trees changing color every day on the adjacent hillsides. And soon the marsh grass turned from a brilliant shimmering deep field of tall green, to a dull golden brown. And he thought back to springtime on the Connecticut, and how he had watched the marsh grass turn from a dull dead off white bunch of sticks, then show subtle signs of color, then continue to mellow through the full spectrum of greens. And he also noticed that the rich, sodden deep brown bank of soil and roots and life, falling off into the river, seemed to always remain the same. And the sound of the kingfisher could be heard, not far off, but he was never seen.

As the water cooled off in the sound, the conch fishing died off in a hurry. "Time for lobsters again," the Codfather announced with a distinguishable tone of excitement in his voice. "At least we don't have to worry about the worms." So they set out the lobster traps again, although not as many as they had set in the summer. "Can't count on getting out every day this time of year, damn northwest winds' gonna blow more often than not now until the seasons make up their mind and fall gives way to winter. In the meantime, we'll keep oystering when we can't get out."

Davey noticed that the weather had done exactly what the Codfather had predicted it would. The northwest wind was damned near relentless. "You gotta watch for the balloons," the Codfather announced calmly, late one morning as he quartered the Novi back towards the harbor in a stiff breeze and a heavy chop. He looked over his shoulder and up above the horizon into a brilliantly crisp blue fall sky. A line of high white large puffy clouds was nearly overhead. "When you see those balloons coming on the horizon, in two hours you're gonna have wind," mark that one well Davey boy. Then the Codfather grasped the wheel tight with both hands and let out a long deep hearty chuckle as he focused on the task of maneuvering the vessel back to port.

And as the seasons struggled in their change, the winds of fall not wanting to give in to the cold calmness of winter, the two fishermen continued to harvest oysters as a steady, reliable source of income. Then in early December the winds over the sound became still as the water became colder. However the lobsters were coming on strong. The Codfather experienced a really productive run right up into the middle of January and then they were gone.

"That's it Davey, time to quit till spring. Waters too cold and the sound is going to sleep. Air's too cold for oystering, no sense in catching 'em', and then having 'em freeze on the deck." So they hauled the traps and stowed the gear and pulled the boats. "I'm headin' for warmer weather for awhile Davey," the Codfather announced to his friend. And with a handshake he was gone.

Davey liked to work with his hands. He also liked lobstering more than any type of fishery that he had been exposed to up to this point in his life, lobstering and gillnetting. He had saved up a considerable amount of money throughout the previous year's hard, busy seasons and now with the Codfather gone for who knows how long, he decided to busy himself with the task of building some new gear for the spring.

Davey had a workshop set up in the old garage behind his grandparents' house. There was no heat or electricity but Davey had made it comfortable and he spent the next two cold months building lobster traps. He worked diligently at the task, weaving his own funnels for hours on end and then putting the traps together. It seemed like a form of artwork, making a fine wooden trap from a bunch of sticks and some nails and a roll of nylon twine.

As the winter wore on, the stack of traps out in the driveway along the wooden fence that ran out to the street grew longer and longer. And not only was that stack of traps growing longer and longer, so were the daylight hours with the approach of spring. Now it came to be the beginning of March and still no Codfather. Davey strung up a couple of gillnets out in the driveway and after that, he was ready to fish.

"Albie, when do you usually set in for lobsters?" Davey had gone to visit his friend. "March fifteenth is the date that I shoot for. Water might still be a little cold but if the traps are there waiting for em when they start to move, you're gonna catch. And in early spring if you know where to find em, and they start potting up, it's like catching gold, because the price for the first run mature hard shell lobsters is way up, sometimes six dollars a pound wholesale. It's like catching gold, dark green and black and orange and yellow gold."

Davey could no longer wait for the Codfather's return. He had to get back out on the sound. He still had the fifteen foot wooden cabin boat, but now he had to make a very important decision, and he thought really long and hard about it. He loved fishing with the Codfather. He was totally confident and at ease when they were on the water together. However, Davey wanted to focus his efforts on lobstering and gillnetting his own bait out on the sound. To Davey, this presented more of a challenge than any other of the fisheries that he had been exposed to at this point in his life, and when the lobsters were running, a greater financial reward if you could 'find 'em.'

Also, deep down inside, Davey wanted to be his own man and make his own decisions. So after a few days of thinking things out, he took a deep breath and told himself that he was going to set off on his own and give it a try. Now for a boat, he thought to himself. I gotta get a bigger and better boat to run all this gear properly, and almost if by magic, he found a beautiful twenty-two foot wooden Oregon dory down town away in Madison. It had been hand crafted by the owner, and had all of the characteristics of a good, seaworthy, inshore Long Island sound fishing boat.

Her high gunwales flared out from the chine boards that held two by six ribs. A two by six rub rail ran from stem to stern and the gunwale was capped off with an additional two by six beam rail. She had a four by four stem that projected up above the bowline, and a slotted wooden deck and a center council. But to Davey, the most intriguing feature to the boat's design was its arching crescent shaped transom and high built in motor well, which in Davey's keen analysis of the vessel, would prevent any chance of taking on water from a following sea.

She was powered by a seventy horsepower Johnson outboard. She also had a six horsepower hauler motor mounted inside the council, a davit, block and long white oak culling board. "All set up for lobstering and gillnetting," Davey thought to himself. Perfect, I gotta have this boat." So he bought the boat and trailer for eighteen hundred dollars 'a steal' he thought to himself.

Then he went up to the State Capital building in Hartford, and bought himself a commercial fishing license and a commercial finfish license for the grand total of two hundred dollars, and in the spring of nineteen-seventy-nine, at the age of twenty-two, Davey set out to make a living on his own on Long Island sound.

"Put an extra brick in the parlor when you set dry traps, otherwise the tide will take 'em who knows where before they soak up and sink." Davey had gone to see Albie for some initial advice. "And set it to uptide from where you want your trap to lie on the bottom. The tide will guide it there for you after awhile. Try to visualize and remember where you set each trap and how you felt how it set up on the bottom, and what was in that trap when you pulled it up, and someday you'll see a pattern and you'll become a successful fisherman.

Davey moored his dory using squatter's rights, between two strong hickory stakes just downstream from the state launching ramp on the Branford river. A couple years back he had acquired a fine fifteen foot canoe as partial payment for working for Harry Johnson, which would become his dinghy. He kept it hidden in the tall pampas grass along the bank. His canoe became the main link between shore and sound, even though the dory lay moored less than a hundred feet from shore.

In the quiet false light before dawn early that April, Davey paddled his canoe out to the dory, fired her up, switched the mooring lines then pulled away and up to the ramp. It was the top of the tide so he brought her right up inside, almost to the head of the ramp, and tied off. Then he proceeded to load the traps from his pickup onto the boat, along with the bait, and he stowed extra equipment in the front compartment just behind the bow. Then he was off. Off for his first set as a commercial fisherman on his own on Long Island sound.

Upon gaining the last bend in the river and making his way down the long reach to the town dock, the sun greeted Davey through the treetops in the land south and east. And that glowing red-orange ball followed him out on his port side, out through the trees, and then exploded with light and warmth on the open sound, as he cleared Johnson's point.

Davey's mind was full of questions. There were so many places to try. When he fished with the Codfather, he always took things for granted. Now it was his turn to read the water and find the fish. He had Bird Rock, Five Foot, Cow and Calf Jeffries, Clam Island, Little Specks, Negro's Heads, Spectacle Island, the Beacon, Townsend Ledge, the Umbrella, where to start he asked himself?

Davey decided to start close, and then eventually work his trap line farther and farther away from the harbor. Pulling up to the Cow and Calf he presently became aware of the fact that there were forty or fifty lobster trap buoys of various colors and configuration surrounding the two rocks that were just awash at the top of the tide. Taking out his chart, he noticed that besides the two rocks that were awash the adjacent reef ran in a northwest direction towards the umbrella islands, which are merely a series or rocks that continue towards shore. Being relatively distant from the large cluster of other traps, Davey strung out the fifteen that he had on the boat on what he figured to be the reef that ran towards the Umbrellas. The next day, out went another fifteen traps, then another and another and another. Then Davey set out one of his gillnets. It produced almost two bushels of menhaden the following morning, as well as a handful of small bluefish and a couple weakfish.

The excitement ran high throughout Davey's body and mind as he pulled up to his first buoy and hauled back on the warp. Man o' man, three beautiful red and black and green and yellow and orange lobsters were nestled in the back of the trap, and one of them gauged out to be a keeper! Davey felt as if he was on top of the world on that cold, bright calm mid-April morning. The inshore spring run was peaking, and Davey was a part of it, and it was awesome. Eventually, Davey extended his trap line in a big circle, with about a two-mile radius, and by mid-May, he had about one hundred and twenty traps in the water. That first spring on his own had many lessons in store for the young fisherman. For the first couple weeks he caught plenty of bait and plenty of lobsters. Then toward the middle of May, most of his traps began to come up empty.

"What's going on?" Davey had called upon the knowledge and wisdom of Albie once again. "They're going into a shed," Albie told his friend. "When the water temperature hits sixty degrees, they find a good place to hide so they're not vulnerable to their many predators until then new shell becomes somewhat firm. Be patient and get ready for an unbelievable experience." Throughout the remainder of May, the lobstering was really slow for Davey. He'd steam out every day and faithfully tend to his traps however his catch was down to about a dozen a day, sometimes even less. He noticed that Albie and the other old-timers were still coming in with descent catch even though they were fishing a lot less gear. Davey became discouraged, yet remained patient and faithful to his task.

Then in the beginning of the third week of June it happened. Overnight, those traps that had been coming up nearly empty for weeks exploded with lobsters of all kinds of colors, shapes, and sizes. Davey couldn't believe it. It was as if there was some big gate down there on the bottom, and all these lobsters had been waiting behind it and suddenly someone or something had opened it up! But after about a week of this bountiful, busy exciting fishery, Davey came into a very disappointing and frustrating situation.

"My gillnet was cut right in half Albie. And each half was all tangled up and sunk to the bottom and full of spider crabs and seaweed. And as for my traps, half of the doors were wide open and some of the entry funnels were all cut up. I never bothered anybody else out there. Albie, and I never got too close to anyone's gear with my own. What the hell is going on?" "Initiation boy, plain and simple." They just want to make sure that you're totally dedicated to it. They're testing your will to survive. Try getting out earlier, like in the predawn light like the rest of us and maybe that'll earn their respect." So from then on, Davey went out really early. And he kept an eye on all of the other boats in his area. And after awhile the harassment diminished to an occasional open door, or a lost trap, which probably could be attributed to some pleasure boater looking for a free lobster dinner or getting a buoy line caught in his prop.

The run lasted through early August. Davey fished hard and made some pretty good money for himself. He also began to associate with the other fishermen in his area, whether it was in passing out on the sound, or shore side on the docks. Davey made an effort to become friendly with the old-timers that fished in his area. At first, only Albie would give him much more than the time of day, but eventually his patient persistence earned the friendship of most of the local lobster men.

He was by far the youngest of the group, but they all knew him from his experiences with the Codfather and because of that fact and because of the way that he displayed a tenacious love and dedication to the inshore trap fishery, he became accepted by most of the group, especially the old-timers. The first season on his own was full of challenges, hard work, excitement and anticipation. During that first season Davey also experienced plenty of apprehension and frustration. However he loved every trip. Every trap that came off the bottom possessed within an enchanting mystery, which was broken when released from the dark swirling clutches of the sound.

The fall run came on in similar fashion as the summer, however much was different. The sound quickly became void of crowded pleasure boat activity. And when the November winds gave way to the cold stillness of winter, lobstering became a peaceful, quiet reflective experience, it became an intimate time for Davey and the sound. In the cold weather, fishing alone, Davey realized the importance of paying attention to everything that he was doing, as well as everything that was going on around him. His senses were on high alert. Every trip, every movement became a one on one experience with his natural environment. And upon arriving back to the safety of the river at the conclusion of each trip he felt proud and thankful and enriched from the experience.

Thick fog blanketed the shoreline on the morning of Davey's first set that following early April. He had waited till about mid-morning for a breeze to push it out, however the air crept out of the river in the eerie pilings lining the river channel.

Upon gaining the faint diffused green flash of the Mermaid light, he heard the dull hum of an oncoming vessel. Banking off to starboard, he steered his dory clear, peering intently into the thick white smoke. Presently another boat came into view, not thirty feet off of Davey's port beam. The approaching vessel was nearly the same color as the fog, dull off-white and only the long wood culling board and grey metal davit gave any indication that this was indeed a manmade object and not part of the fog itself.

A man in faded orange oilskins and a salt and pepper beard and a black Greek fisherman's cap and a smoking pipe clenched between his lips pulled up alongside. Davey immediately noticed that there were two wire baskets full of big, fresh glistening lobsters on the deck behind the man. He was mystified by the situation. How could this man have fished all morning under these conditions and brought home such a fine catch?

"Canoe, you got a compass? Trust your compass. Maybe you're a little crazy canoe, crazy like me, or maybe you just love the water and fishing, like me, just remember, you're compass doesn't lie."

He pushed off and quickly disappeared in the fog, but before he disappeared Davey noticed the black letters fading in the swirling mist "My Bunny."

"Just keep her at two ten," Davey said to himself, and you'll hit the Cow and Calf; maybe a couple degrees less now and then to allow for the incoming. To Davey, steaming out in the fog was an awesome natural event that held very surrealistic and supernatural characteristics. The surface of the water and the fog seemed to be one and the same. Neither seemed to have a beginning or an end. It seemed as if he was moving through an endless tunnel that held no boundaries, with the feeling that the end could be anywhere just ahead.

Suddenly the red bell buoy with the numbers "thirty four" seemed to float towards him in the fog. Feeling a great sense of satisfaction and pride, Davey turned off to the northwest and set his traps on the reef that ran in that direction towards shore. And that's the way it was for the lobster fisherman during that period of time on Long Island sound. It was a simple way of life without all of today's modern technology. They used their compass and shore ranges to navigate and the old timers used sounding irons to get a feel for the depth and condition of the bottom, and seemingly everyone that was involved had an intimate relationship with the wind and waves and tide.

Davey loved the never ending challenge. Each day on his way down the river in the predawn light, he'd formulate a game plan in where to start his circle and where to end it. It all depended on what nature had in store for him on any given day. He had to plan to work with it, to go with the flow and try to choose the path of least resistance, however sometimes the conditions could quickly change, and he would have to change his strategy. Davey got into a smooth rhythm, coming up to the buoy into the wind or tide, depending on which was presently the stronger force, then he'd snag the line just below the surface with his boat hook and simultaneously cut the wheel to port and take it out of gear. At that point he would fetch up the buoy then pull in enough slack in order to slip the rope over the pulley at the end of the davit then pull it down and wrap a turn and a half on the spinning drum of the hauler motor and draw the trap until it broke water, then he'd grab it with his right hand and at the same time, he'd let slack off of the hitch on the spinning drum and whip the line free. Then continuing this one fluid motion he'd pull the trap up and onto and sideways onto the long narrow oak culling board.

Then he'd quickly clean out the trap throwing the conch into one basket and fish into another. And the spider crabs and native crabs and starfish and kelp and seaweed and small lobsters went back into the sound. Any potential keeper lobsters were placed right on top of the counsel. Then while steaming back up into the tide, he'd empty the bait bag, grab a full one, hook it in place on the nail in the top of the middle frame, facing the front of the trap, then secure the door. When he felt that the time was right, he'd turn the trap sideways on the culling board; push it over end first, then quickly cut the wheel to starboard as the line paid out. When the line was just about ready to go taut, he'd toss the buoy overboard and move on to the next trap. On the way he'd band up the claws of any keepers and put them in a basket port-side, covered with wet burlap bags. Weather permitting, he could run the circle in four or five hours and pull seventy or eighty traps. If the wind kicked up and blew hard, the challenge grew greater and the task more strenuous and time consuming. Only a strong wind and an angry sea kept him from steaming out on a daily basis.

Mid-April typically brought a steady run of egg laden menhaden migrating northward through the sound, just offshore. And this year was no different. At first, usually once fish moved in, they became a reliable source of lobster bait in the gillnets throughout the spring, through summer and even into mid to late fall. This species would fan out into their traditional brackish water estuaries to spawn, and then spend the remainder of the warm water months feeding on plankton spawned from local creeks and marshes. However in the first week of May, the nets were coming up nearly empty. The traps needed bait, Davey sought the advice of Albie. "Meet me out at five foot rock at sunset, bring your lantern boxes and your gillnets and a sleeping bag, and maybe we'll catch some bait." Davey was there and ready at the red nun that marked five foot rock, a small boulder filled reef that lies about a mile offshore almost straight outside the harbor. Albie was there waiting at anchor along with the Cigar man in his tiny wooden skiff. Davey pulled up alongside Albie and tied off.

"How many nets you got?" Albie asked Davey. "Three, I got three one hundred footers, two three inch mesh and one three and a half." "Well here's what you do. Steam south until you hit a "scum line." I don't know what causes it, maybe a change on the bottom or maybe its just the way the tide runs, but you'll find one. There's seaweed and those small orange jellyfish and lots of brown algae and lots of manmade trash floating along in it. But God only knows the reason, they attract fish. Set your lantern box and tie your nets to it, and tie them all together and tie them off to your bow, and I'll see you in the morning."

Albie, Davey, and the Cigar man went their separate ways, slowly fanning out southward. Davey noticed the brown line of foam not a quarter mile from the nun. In the growing darkness, he saw the Cigar man's lantern set in off to the west, then Albie's, about a quarter mile east of the first lantern. Davey steamed east in the scum slick for a bit, to allow enough distance from the other fishermen so as not to interfere with their space, then set his lantern box and his nets in.

When darkness came, he thought of rowing all night to keep the net taut, like he did with the Codfather while shad fishing on the Connecticut river. However when looking out upon the faint outline of Albie's boat and the Cigar man's boat, he saw only that, and the faint glow of their lanterns gently bobbing on the nearly calm surface. So he laid out his sleeping bag on the deck, crawled in, looked up at the clear early night sky and watched it fill up with stars, and went to sleep.

When he awoke, it was light. It was early and quiet but it was light. He stood up, the evening still a dim memory of his recent past. Albie was not far off to the west, hauling in his net, and the Cigar man not far beyond him doing the same. Davey could see the shining thrashing forms of fish in their nets as they came out of the water and over the gunwale. Then he looked out beyond his own bow and he was shocked to see nothing but water. No lantern box, no top water buoys, nothing. He went up to the bow and untied the buoy line and started to pull back. The nets were still there. They'd been drawn beneath the surface by the weight of his catch. It was incredible. It seemed as if every mesh held a mackerel.

It took Davey nearly three hours to pull in his catch, and when he was done. The entire deck was covered with mackerel, along with all of the fish boxes and baskets that he had on board. On his way back to the ramp, he stopped at the town float and gave some fish to anyone that wanted some. He just wanted to share the bounty in some little manner.

Towards mid-May, Davey noticed something unusual happening. Up to this point and time everyone that was lobstering in his area had traditionally fished the reefs and around the islands and rocks along the shoreline. No one ever strayed further out into the sound much further than maybe a half mile south of the Branford reef which lies about two and one half miles off shore.

Presently however, Davey noticed a few of the lobstermen upon tending their traps, were stacking them up on the decks of their vessels and steaming offshore. Davey thought back to that foggy morning meeting with "My Bunny" and all of those nice lobsters that the fisherman had on board.

"Albie, that boat 'My Bunny,' you know that guy?" Davey had to find out. "Yeah, that's Vinnie the pirate; he keeps her down behind the factory, way upstream, just below the bridge. He's got a little shack back amongst the old brick buildings where he builds his gear. He don't talk to nobody, but people been findin' out his secrets. He fishes offshore, right out to the middle of the sound, maybe even further, and he comes back with more lobsters than anybody's ever seen around here. Now the other fishermen are moving out there as well, takin' up the grounds." "I'm gonna go for it," Davey told Albie, in a determined and serious tone. "Be careful, it's a whole different world out there," replied his long time friend.

Chapter 8

Canoe

Davey had an established fishery of around two hundred traps, covering an area of about four square miles. However the reality was that he could have fished half that number on the spread out relatively small productive areas and probably would have caught just as many lobsters. So in late May, when the fishing got really slow before the shedder run, he kept a load of traps on the boat and steamed south to see what he could find. He was amazed at the number of buoys being pulled in the tide starting about three miles offshore and seemingly running in a southerly direction. He steamed between a line of white buoys with black numbers, and orange and white ones and set his traps parallel to the two lines. Thus he began his move offshore.

The line grew longer. Soon it was sixty traps long, and when he pulled the line for the first time, there were lobsters, more lobsters than he had ever caught before in sixty traps. Then there became two lines, then three. Davey was catching good, however many other things were happening in the meantime. The other fishermen who had moved their gear offshore started getting bigger boats and fishing bigger, heavier gear, rigged in three trap trawls. Vinnie appeared on the grounds with the "Lobster Lady," a beautiful thirty-one-foot cedar planked, oak framed Jonesport Maine boat powered by a four-fifty-four Chrysler gas engine that he had personally steamed back from down East Maine. Then there was Nick who previously owned a twenty-four foot beamy wooden scow. He showed up with a thirty-six-foot wooden Nova

Scotia hull, the "Ramona B." Then came Buddy B, who had parted with his ancient nineteen-foot wooden Lyman lap strake for a thirty-four-foot battleship of fishing boats. She was built by the Wilcox boat builders in New London, Connecticut. She boasted a five quarter square mahogany planked hull, each piece being routed with a three quarter half round bit, so that one plank laid inside of the next. These planks were fixed to a heavy oak frame and stringers. "Mr. Starbuck" was the name stenciled on either side of her ebony hull. Then came Anthony on the forty-two-foot wooden monster "Betty C," and Bart came out with a thirty-four-foot Novi, a lightly built boat with white pine planks and cedar frame, scrambling for space, steaming from nearby New Haven harbor. Finally there was D.J. who methodically got into position with his ancient; thirty-foot Beals Island built "Bug Catcher." Then there was "Canoe." Canoe had his dory, and now he was out in the middle of the "big pond," surrounded by big boats and big gear.

"Canoe, you gotta move those traps," Vinnie had steamed alongside Davey as he made his way up his west line. "They're too light for out here in the deep water and they drift into every-one else's gear and your buoys are too small, they get sucked under in a strong tide and the other guys, along with myself are getting your unseen lines caught up in our `props. Move down to the east," Vinnie advised the young man, "there's more room down there and just as many lobsters, they just come a little later that's all."

Unfortunately, Davey didn't take Vinnie's advice. He was catching real good and he was stubborn and competitive; he be-came a thorn in the side of the other lobstermen in the area. He tried his best, the lobsters were there, however he couldn't always get out to the offshore grounds in the dory, and when he couldn't, he paid the price. Missing traps, no lobsters, traps busted up so bad that they had to be taken ashore for repair, those were some of the consequences of his stubbornness. He heard the talk on shore, on the docks. That damned Canoe, his gear is all over the place messin' everyone up.

Davey wasn't ready to accept the inevitable. Every time that he got out to the offshore grounds, he always pulled up at least a few traps that held a rich bounty of big beautiful lobsters. However, when mid-August arrived and it was time to pull in his traps for worm season, reality set in. From his original number of two-hundred and forty traps that he had brought offshore, he was only able to retrieve one-hundred and thirty-five.

Davey had to weigh the odds in regards to his fall lobstering effort. Now that he had time to take a break from the busy summer run, he had to try to put the whole event into perspective. After days of deliberation and contemplation, as well as much reflection, he came to a conclusion. He decided to go back to his old way of fishing the inshore grounds. The reality, he concluded was that his boat and gear were too small for the task of fishing the offshore grounds. Also, the other guys lobstering out there weren't making it easy for him to survive.

So Davey prepared his traps that he had stored on the barge next to Albie's and Brooksies' and the Cigar Man's. Then one day in mid-October as Davey was easing his canoe up into the pampas grass alongside the southern bulkhead of the state ramp, Vinnie stepped out onto the narrow pier. "Canoe, I got a proposition for you, he said after taking the smoking pipe from his mouth. Come down to my dock when you get done, maybe we can work something out." Then he was gone. Davey pulled his canoe up into the tall grass alongside the pier then loaded up his old Ford pickup. On his way out of the parking lot and down Harbor street, he thought about what Vinnie might have to offer him. As he neared the turnoff that leads down to Vinnie's dock, he thought "what the heck, it won't hurt to go and see what's on his mind."

As he pulled in, he spotted a plume of smoke rising from behind a stack of drying wooden traps. Vinnie was on the other side, mending gear, "Canoe, I'm lookin' for a stern man on the Lobster Lady. I'm fishin' a lot of gear, four-hundred and fifty traps, and trawl fishing is a lot different than fishing singles. You could still run your nets and fish the inside on your own as we'll be done early and when we get in, you'll be free to go. I'll pay you fifty dollars a day for your help. Its two lines a day, twenty-five three-trap trawls out then the same back in. When the run's on and we're catching heavy, I'll take care of you," he added. "Come on down and check out the boat," Vinnie added as he headed down the old long narrow wooden ramp.

The Lobster Lady was a beauty. She was Vinnie's pride and joy and he kept her spotless. Her powdered blue hull was planked so tight and painted so fine it looked like fiberglass rather than cedar. Her wide gunwales were white oak and her deck was strip planked tongue and groove fir, both of which gave off a rich grainy luster thanks to the new coat of linseed oil that Vinnie had just applied. Her superstructure consisted of a fairly roomy "V" birth cabin and behind that was the three paned windshield, a glass pane about three feet long on the port side of the dashboard which was a flat surface about two feet deep that held the helm and electronics and compass and a brass lever that ran the hydraulic pump motor for the pulling drum, a low wooden roof allowed Vinnie just enough headroom to stand erect and extended back about four feet from the front of the dashboard.

Vinnie had been lobstering for more than thirty years, and had worked hard to be able to afford this big new vessel. Davey thought to himself that it would be an honor to work with the first fisherman in Branford to explore the offshore waters. "What time do we leave?" he asked, trying to hold back his excitement. "Be down the dock by four-thirty tomorrow morning." Vinnie replied, while trying to hold back his own excitement. Now the two lone fishermen both had company.

Vinnie was quiet at first. He smoked his pipe "Irish Mist," he announced, although Davey had never questioned the contents of the bowl. The smoke from his pipe left a constant mellow fragrance that lingered in the small shelter offered by the windows and roof, Vinnie drove the boat, and Davey stood next to him, leaning his elbows on the edge of the dashboard. The warm purr of the Buick under the wooden box between them, separated them, but at the same time, drew them together. It was Vinnie, the old captain with the tattered Greek fisherman's cap, smoking his pipe looking out into the water. And it was the young man full of excitement and anticipation, upon this new endeavor. And it was the "Lobster Lady," the solid work horse which Vinnie handled with an experienced, masterful smoothness.

Vinnie showed Davey the ropes, calmly and thoroughly, step by step. He always stressed the importance of keeping one's eye on the lines on the deck. Davey had the responsibility of tending to the first two traps of the three pot trawls, cleaning them out and rebating them, then slinging them down the gunwale and onto the stern. Vinnie would tend to the third trap and usually Davey would be quick enough to jump in and help him, changing the bait bag and taking over the clean up while Vinnie maneuvered the boat back in line with the rest of the trawls.

Then when the time was right, Vinnie would spin the lead trap at right angles to the gunwale and push it overboard. Then he'd steam, and the rope on the deck would pay out, then hop up over the stern and pull the second trap into the white foamy wash, then another coil of rope would pay out and become taut and the third trap would spring overboard. Then the buoy line would pay out and just before it went taut Vinnie would throw they buoy overboard in a manner that caused it to land flat, softly slapping the surface of the sound.

Atop the engine box there were two wooden fish boxes. One held a small plastic tub full of lobster bands for the claws, and the plier-like banding tool. The keeper lobsters were placed in the other box. On the way to the next trawl, Davey would quickly band up the lobsters and toss them into the live tank which was fed constant water by the wash down pump and stood mid-ships up against the port gunwale. There were two wire bushel baskets on the deck just behind the holding tank; one was for marketable fish, and the other for conch.

Both fishermen loved the experience, and they worked very hard to succeed at their task. Every sunrise, every rising trap held a special mystery and energy of its own. For the fishermen, this was the essence of life itself. Being out on the sound day in and day out, soaking up the sun's warm midmorning warmth and energy and light, and watching its light energy come alive on the surface of the water in millions of sparkling diamonds dancing on a light breeze, or watching clouds form into misty mare's tails in a clear, bright June sky, or battling an outgoing tide on an east wind in a driving gray rainstorm. Vinnie had a strong connection with the sound and its environment, and it rubbed off quickly on Davey, and their time spent together on the Lobster Lady was always filled with awesome, seemingly out of body energy.

Davey's youthfulness and enthusiasm soon rubbed off on Vinnie. He became like a young man again, that had long been dormant in the silence of loneliness. The shiny smiling twinkle in his squinting eyes, and his comical nature made every trip fun. When the weather was good, Vinnie had that manner about him all day, however when it was rough, he was cautiously apprehensive in regards to their safety and saved the joking around for the long steam home.

It was mid-July and they were catchin' real good, about four-hundred pounds a day for that matter, when one day on their steam home, Vinnie became serious and started to talk. "You see Canoe," he began; there are two different populations of lobsters in the sound. First there are the native dark green and black and dark orange shells that live mostly along the shoreline on the reefs and in the rocks. This native population migrates to cooler, deeper waters in the summertime and back again inshore come late fall. You see, out here, the bottom of the sound isn't flat, like you might think it is. It's like a series of ridges that run east to west that drop off deeper and deeper into the sound the farther you go out. And along the vertical part of these ridges, the lobsters burrow into the bank like honeycombs in a bee's nest, then back themselves in and wait for a meal to go by. They're also scavengers and wait till night to venture out and prowl along the flats in search of food. That's how the native population lives and thrives in the sound. They'll survive on barnacles from the reefs in early spring, and then thrive on native crabs and small fish or just about anything the rest of the year when the sound is alive."

"Then there's the migratory summer population that streams into the sound with the warm ocean currents and the abundance of marine life that comes with the flow." "See the lobsters in our tank. Notice how bright and varied their colors. We've caught calicos, yellows, bright greens, bright oranges and reds and blacks and any combination of all of those. That run is from the ocean, from the Gulf Stream, the life pulse of summer out here in the sound. Notice that how in the summer we see a variety of unusual creatures out here in mid-sound as well as many unusual occurrences. Take the bluefish for example. Come late June out in the middle, there'll be acres upon acres of bluefish finning on the water's surface. They won't bite on anything during this time because they're spawning, and to my knowledge I've never heard of anyone landing a bluefish with roe in its belly. Then come the different varieties of jellyfish, and green sea turtles and bonito and the occasional ocean sunfish to name a few. I've even seen dolphin out here; they all flow in the warm currents of summer's life stream. And you'll see different birds out here as well; all in the trip of this primordial nomadic natural force. Davey, I pioneered the offshore fishery in Branford and now many have followed and the grounds are crowded. This good fishing ain't gonna last forever. Next year we're gettin' a New York state license and we're goin' on the other side of the pond."

That first year with Vinnie was just solid fishing for Davey. He kept his inshore line although he had reduced the number of traps down to about eighty. He'd fish offshore with Vinnie all morning, and then he'd go out on his own boat in the afternoon and pull his nets and traps. He just couldn't get enough of being out on the sound.

The following spring, Vinnie had a new plate on the side of the Lobster Lady's cabin: "NY1163." During the course of the winter he had also made some larger traps. They began setting out the trawls on April fifteenth. Davey had already been fishing for a month, and he was doing pretty well since native lobsters were scarce and the price was still way up. At six dollars a pound wholesale, a bushel was worth about one-hundred and eighty dollars. They would bring out fifteen trawls at a time. Davey would drive the "Lady," while Vinnie executed the initial set. Vinnie wanted to make sure that everything went off just right. After they had established their two west lines, Vinnie switched to a different tactic. They started bringing out then trawls and fifteen singles, those big new traps with long lines and oversized buoys. They'd slowly set in their trawls, then making sure that no other boats were in sight they'd steam south, across the unseen but charted boundary into New York waters.

Vinnie had a Loran; all of the lobstermen were getting Loran's, a digitally charted grid system of navigation. Mid-sound is the seventy line "13970" on the north/south grid. Every ten digits represent a one point one mile reach. They stopped at the forty-seven line. Other buoys could be seen in the distance. They appeared to be running east to west. Vinnie and Davey set in their singles accordingly on the forty-seven line.

After the fourth set in New York waters it was time to haul up the first forty-five singles. Vinnie and Davey anxiously peered into the clear dark blue water as the first trap made the one hundred and twenty foot ascent from the bottom. The trap held lobsters, big lobsters with crusher claws the size of tomahawks! Out of those forty-five traps they boated almost four bushels of select lobsters averaging almost two pounds each, with a handful in the three to four pound range! This was far and above any catch probably ever seen in Connecticut waters for forty-five traps.

Vinnie had done it again. He was the first fisherman from Branford, maybe even from the whole Connecticut shoreline for that matter to venture out to the other side of the sound and harvest its rich bounty of lobsters.

Soon Vinnie and Davey had two lines of sixty singles in New York waters. Their southernmost line was almost twelve miles from the Connecticut shoreline and about four miles from the north shore of Long Island, New York. For a few weeks the two fishermen made some phenomenal catches from those big offshore traps, however nothing lasts forever.

One morning upon reaching the beginning of their northern New York line, they sensed right away that something was wrong. It was a bright, clear calm dawn, and typically they could see the long, straight evenly spaced large white buoys with the thin oak stick protruding from the top bobbing and swaying in the current with their black stamped numbers "1163" stretching out as far as the eye could see. However this morning the buoys were few and far between and scattered all over the place.

As they began hauling the traps, they noticed a large, maybe forty-five foot white fishing boat steaming in their direction from the south, while at the same time, an even larger dark blue boat with long steel outriggers and a big steel drum, obviously a stern dragger, steamed towards them from the east. "We got company Canoe," Vinnie announced calmly to Davey. "Just be calm and let me do the talking."

The two boats converged at very close quarters on the "Lobster Lady." Vinnie took the boat out of gear and calmly stepped out on the back deck drawing deeply and slowly from the ever-present tobacco pipe. "What the hell is this gear doing on our side of the sound? Your home port is in Connecticut, and that's where you should be fishing. No one else ever wandered over here so who in hell do you think you are?" A burly middle-aged man with a heavy beard and fire in his eyes was expressing his anger over the situation from the deck of the white lobster boat. Vinnie remained calm and quiet as the captain of the dragger started in on him.

"Your gear is right in the middle of my dragging lane, between the forty-eight and forty-five," he loudly exclaimed, hands waving wildly in the air. We got this all set up over here on our side of the pond, some areas are reserved for dragging lanes and the rest is for trap fishing, and there's no fuckin' room for any more gear."

"Them traps ain't movin'," Vinnie announced to the two captains in a calm but stern voice. "I've been fishing this sound for over thirty years, I paid for my license, it's a free ocean, and I'm gonna fish wherever the fuck I want to fish." With that being said Vinnie returned to the helm and continued on his way, searching out the scattered gear and straightening out the line.

After that encounter, their efforts in regards to fishing in New York waters became less and less successful. Although there were never any more direct encounters with the New York fishermen, the gear was always scattered about and broken up and more and more traps disappeared. Then one mid-morning while they were patching up their for-five line, a call came to them on the V.H.F. radio. It was a faint staticy voice. "Lobster Lady, you out there, come in Lobster Lady." Vinnie grabbed the microphone from the stainless steel clip on the side of the radio. "Lobster Lady here, go ahead."

"Vinnie its Allie down here to the West, good storm a comin', lots of wind at first then heavy rain and lots of electricity. If you're close, get in, if you're not, get ready." "Thanks Al," Vinnie replied, and then he put the mic back on the clip.

Davey looked around. He couldn't see land anywhere. It wasn't the first time on the water that he felt open and vulnerable, however at this point he felt those feelings more than ever. "What are we gonna do Cap?" he asked Vinnie, who had continued to work up the line, seemingly unconcerned regarding the approach of what sounded like a very nasty thunderstorm. "These traps need fresh bait, so that's what we're gonna do. We're gonna' tend to these traps."

To the west, Davey could see the black sky and streaks of lightening drawing quickly closer. Then came the wind, and with it a dark high rolling sea, capped with blowing white foam. Suddenly they were engulfed in an eerie lime green cloud. Visibility was reduced to almost zero and rain came in a torrential wind driven downpour. Sometimes out on the sound, the rain nocks the wind down and the sea goes flat calm. However presently this was not the case. The rain was no match for the intensity of this storm. Then came the lightning and thunder. Bolts of lightning flashed often and close, illuminating the green cloud that had engulfed them with a bright powerful almost blinding flash. And the thunder that followed, many times often simultaneously, shook the "Lady" and humbled Davey.

Vinnie didn't say a word, although his face had taken on a sudden paleness, he remained calm. He slowly brought the "Lady" about, carefully maneuvering her into the deep troughs and over the cresting swells, until he had brought the bow directly into the wind. Then, in the fury of the raging storm, he slowly idled the "Lady" into the wind and huge sea with one hand on the wheel and the other clutching the smoking pipe trapped between his jaw, which was producing a steady plume of smoke that seemed to engulf his whole head.

Davey was really scared for his life. He went down into the cabin, got into a fetal position on the starboard wooden bunk and pulled some old rain gear over his body and his head. It seemed as if the storm was never going to end. Vinnie kept the "Lady's" bow steady into the wind. She wasn't pounding, however Davey could feel her riding up, almost vertical, and over the huge waves, then sliding down into the trough on the backside. Davey thought for sure that it was time to meet his maker. He thought surely that one of the brilliant flashes of electricity was bound to hit the boat and splinter it into a million pieces. He wasn't worried about being overcome by the wind and waves, as Vinnie was handling the "Lady" with experienced courage. It was the blinding flash of lightening and deafening closeness of thunder that completely humiliated the young fisherman.

Gradually the bright flashes grew dimmer, and the rattling reverberations of the ensuing thunder echoed softer and ever farther to the east. Then the rain slowed to a drizzle on the cabin roof, and the sky became brighter, and the "Lady's" steep up and down pitch gradually became more subdued.

Davey sat up on the wooden berth, threw the rubber coverings off to the side and just sat there for a minute, elbows on legs, hands cradling his head. Then he got up and came out of the cabin onto the deck, and resumed his position on the port side of the engine box and rested his arms on the console. He didn't look at Vinnie, nor did Vinnie look at "Canoe." "Let's go home," were the only words spoken between the two as the captain pointed the "Lady" to the north and began the long steam back to port.

In what seemed like no time at all, it was again mid-August, worm season, time to haul the traps back to shore. The Connecticut gear was pretty much intact, save for a trawl missing here or there, or one trap occasionally missing from a trawl, however the New York gear was a disaster. Out of the one-hundred and twenty traps that they had set out in the "deep water," only seventy-two came back to the dock.

In the fall, with the weather being quite unpredictable, and those balloon clouds on the horizon in advance of a stiff northwest wind becoming more and more present, Vinnie decided to stay on "his side of the pond." They didn't even set out all of the gear. They only went out twenty trawls on each line. Vinnie had great respect for the sound, knowing how quickly the conditions could change, especially in the fall. In the fall, they couldn't count on getting out every day. Sometimes after a two of three day blow, they'd catch a couple of good days and get out and pull as much gear as they could. Sometimes they'd get "caught up," and wouldn't go out, even if the weather was ideal.

Davey continued to run his own gear, and now that he was occasionally getting "good fishing" days off, he decided that he'd "load up" the Branford reef with traps and try to fish through the winter. Come December, Davey had sixty traps out on the big reef, along with another sixty covering his traditional grounds. Vinnie pulled his gear in the second week of December, after a short but very successful fall run. Now Davey was on his own.

In late fall and into early winter, the native population of lobsters in the sound, migrate to the safety and security of the inshore reefs and rocks, and along the edges of the rocky islands which are scattered along the shoreline, in anticipation of their winter dormancy. Just after Thanksgiving, the price of lobsters goes up for several reasons. First, the offshore run is usually coming to a close, and secondly, not too many people eat turkey for Christmas.

The December calm had set in. Davey was on his own with a lot of gear in the water, and that good run that he had experienced offshore with Vinnie was marching its way right into Davey's gear. He caught really good right up till a few days before Christmas, then came the big freeze.

An extremely cold dry arctic blast brought nearly two inches of clear ice to the harbor and up into the river overnight. Davey had previously been cautioned by many of the old-timers to never try to break through ice of that thickness with a wooden boat. They had warned him that that clear thin ice can cut right through a wooden hull as clean as a razor. Again Davey was at the mercy of Mother Nature, and it just got colder and colder. The ice in the river and harbor became thicker ant thicker each night and extended further and further out into the sound.

One morning Davey took a ride down to Linden avenue in Pawson Park. There's a high bluff and the road runs right along the edge, offering a commanding view of the sound where his gear was set. He couldn't believe what he saw. The sound had frozen all the way out to the Branford reef, and the open water beyond let off a cold frosty mist.

Davey waited anxiously for a chance to retrieve his gear, however the bitter cold weather held and the ice held, and there was nothing that he could do about it except accept it and hunker down and build himself some new gear. Finally there came a January thaw. It took four days for the harbor and river to open up, but on January twenty-second, with a clear calm morning sky, Davey was able to get out.

About an hour into the outgoing tide, a huge mass of ice in the harbor broke free, and was pulled out into the open sound. Then smaller sections of ice broke free in the river channel. They formed a glistening white procession and drifted out with the tide. Davey navigated through the small channel in the river and out of the harbor into a sea filled with thick chunks of drifting ice ranging in size from about as big as his boat, to perhaps the size of a small barge. These frigid obstacles made navigation slow and tricky.

Davey couldn't believe how bright everything was. The snow covered landscape glistened like millions of tiny sparkling diamonds and the ice flows beamed a reflection of the bright gleam of the morning sun.

Upon achieving the broadness of the open sound, Davey could see dozens of large, football field sized ice flows scattered about, marching east in the outgoing tide. Furthermore, the sound, for a far as he could see was scattered with smaller drifting chunks of ice.

He made it to the Branford reef, where three weeks earlier seventy of his traps lay peacefully on the bottom. Now only a scattered handful of icy white buoys could be seen. Davey began pulling up his gear. The gas hauler had frozen up so he pulled by hand. The slotted wooden floorboards froze into a sheet of ice after only a couple of traps had come aboard and shed water onto the deck. Davey had eight traps on the boat, and then upon looking around, with the boat at idle drifting with the tide and the ice, he couldn't see anymore of his little white five by ten buoys. "Damn," he said out loud, "I've lost just about everything." He could see "D.J." in the Bug Catcher off to the southeast. D.J. was one of the few fishermen in Branford that fished year round. It seemed as if he was wandering around aimlessly looking for lost gear. Davey headed out toward the "Bug Catcher," maybe "D.J." had seen some of his gear, he hoped. Then, way out to the east, Davey saw the black hull of the "Mister Starbuck," steaming in the general direction of Davey and "D.J." All three boats met upon that desolate morning, with the frigid mist coming off the cold calm sea, and the ice flows drifting about. It was like three daring adventurers meeting out in the middle of nowhere.

"You got a lot of gear down towards Faulkner's," Bud announced the good news to Davey. "And there's some of your stuff down there too "D.J." The buoys had frozen up in the ice, and when it broke, initially in huge sections, the gear got dragged down to the east in the flows. "Canoe, what the hell are you doing out here? Get your ass back inside what the hell are you crazy or what? You're out here in this, in an open boat with no radio, no nothing, if you get wet, you're gonna freeze to death." "I love the adventure," Davey answered Buddy calmly, "Besides I gotta round up my gear."

"Well, I'm heading in, and I ain't watchin' out for you any more today, but you better hustle up because when the tide starts to come back in, chances are that the river and harbor are gonna get chocked back up with ice."

"I'm headin' down to the east for a while Canoe," D.J. said to Davey. "I'll keep an eye on you." So the three fishermen parted, and continued on their separate, frigid journeys. Faulkners island lies about seven miles east, a little southeast of the Branford reef. As Davey headed off in that direction he would be encountering deeper waters and a stronger tide. About halfway to the island he began to spot some of his gear. The buoys were all gouged up by the ice, as if some giant frozen hand with razor-like fingernails had stubbornly released its grip.

Soon Davey had reclaimed a light load of sixteen traps and began the long steam back to Branford harbor. The weather held; no wind, a bright blue sky, and temperature probably in the low thirties. Most of the harbor around the main channel was free of ice. The river channel was open to a width of about forty feet. At this point it was half tide, still going out. Davey knew that he had more gear down by Faulkners, however he didn't know when he'd be able to get out again. Just before he reached the town dock he made an abrupt turn and headed for the adjacent beach. He had been thinking the whole situation over very carefully during his half hour steam back to port. The tide was still going out. If he went up river and tried to unload onto the barge, chances were that the ice around it was still there, furthermore the tide was getting too low to hastily offload his traps onto its dilapidated metal deck.

Davey steamed directly to the middle of the beach and put the dory hard aground. Quickly he dragged the heavy, frozen moss covered traps above the high tide mark and stacked them on the beach. He then pushed the dory back into the sea jumped on the bow and upon achieving the helm, bolted back out into the sound.

He had worked hard building his gear and he knew that he had seventy feet of buoy line on those traps. The waters just west and south of Faulkners drop off to over seventy feet in many places. Davey figured that the only chance that he would have of ever seeing those buoys again was presently upon him, as the outgoing tide ran slack and the water would be at its most shallow level.

"D.J." was on his way in with a boat load of frozen traps clogged with brown sea moss. "What the hell are you doin' now

Canoe? You crazy bastard." "I got more gear down to the east, and I'm damned well gonna try to get it right now, or maybe never," Davey answered, as he drifted away from the "Bug Catcher." "Good luck, you're on your own," 'D.J' replied with a wave, while shaking his head from side to side in an attempt to make Davey change his plans.

Davey made it down close to Faulkners again. He located another dozen of his traps and got them safely aboard. Then the tide started coming back in, and the ice started flowing back to the west. Davey remembered Bud's warning that the harbor might sock back in again with ice on the incoming tide. He made a half circle to the southwest before heading back to port and picked up four more stray traps in the black water and white ice.

The ice was chocking up the river channel and most of the harbor when Davey finally rounded second point, so he made a bee-line toward the beach. He couldn't get up the river, so he beached the dory again and said to himself, "At least I'm home." He unloaded the gear, stacking it alongside the first frozen load. When he was done, realizing that there was no-where else to go, he ran a long heavy line from the bow and tied it off to the grey metal railing at the head of the beach. His dory and his gear would lie there for another week, frozen testament to a winter far worse than only the old timers could ever remember.

The following spring brought many changes to the sound, most of which were unnatural ones. Everything started out as usual although Davey had a lot less gear to set out. Towards the middle of April he got a visit from Vinnie, "Canoe, I'm gonna fish a lot more gear this year, I'll pay you more money but it's gonna be a long day."

"You're tellin' me that I won't have time to fish my own gear, to do my own thing?" Davey replied.

"Yeah Canoe, that's about the size of it. Everyone's gettin' bigger boats and are gonna be fishin' a lot more gear, wire traps that won't have to come out for worm season. The offshore competition is gettin' tougher and tougher, and there are only so many lobsters out there.

Davey told Vinnie that he'd have to think about it, but he'd get back to him as soon as he'd made his decision. With that Vinnie was gone and Davey was by himself. It was a beautiful calm sun-filled mid-April morning, he was all caught up and cleaned up and packed up and ready to go pedal his catch, however he needed time to think out his options regarding the upcoming season. He walked out to the edge of the pier and sat down. First he looked around close. The water in front of him was ebbing, swirling in the change of tide. Then he looked across the river, out onto the lush green expanse of idle eelgrass, streams of water running ever so discretely from its edge, and disappearing into the brown sodden bank. Then he noticed that a small group of seagulls had formed in the small cove across the river just to his south. They were swimming back and forth along the water's edge and occasionally one of them would strike its head below the surface of the water and violently shake it back and forth. There'd be a mud covered quahog in its beak more often than not. The bird would then proceed to fly over to the adjacent dock to the south, drop its catch and study it for a minute. It would proudly parade around the clam, almost as if it were proud of its accomplishment. Then it would grasp the clam in its beak, vault vertically directly above the middle of the pier and release the clam in an attempt to crack open its rock-like shell. To Davey's amazement after the third or fourth time, and after the bird achieving a greater and greater altitude, he could hear the hollow sound of the shell cracking open. Then the bird would leisurely consume the contents of its catch. Then it would fly over and perch atop one of the many pilings that line the river channel. Then it would look all around for a moment, then nod it's head up and down for a moment as if saying "thanks," then disappear into the sky amidst the masts of a thousand sailboats, peacefully nodding in the tide at their moorings.

Davey wondered in amazement as to how they'd learned to do that. "I suppose it's handed down," he said out loud to himself. Just like lots of things get handed down in nature and in regards to mankind. And he also supposed that it took the unselfish percentage of any given species to have the unique capability to share of itself, or oneself for that matter.

Davey stood up in confidence that he had made his decision. Many unselfish fishermen, and people in general for that matter had handed down to him a great deal of knowledge in regards to commercial fishing, and had stressed the importance of being able to share life's experiences and one's personal knowledge with other people in a way that could possibly make someone's life richer and fuller. Davey decided that for the immediate point in his future, and for whatever amount of time that would pass until some other physical, mental, or emotional obstacle came his way, that he would maintain his personal, simple fishing routine, and in his spare time become a helper.

"Vin, I'll help you get your gear set in, but after that I'm gonna' have to go my own way. Maybe I'll be able to help you out a bit during the summer run, but I wanna keep doin' my own thing, havin' my own boat and gear and all."

"Yeah, Canoe, I understand, I wish that it could be like the old days when you could make a livin' with a couple hundred traps, but we're just gettin' caught up in the times, and I'm just trying' to keep up with the competition."

"Yeah Vin I hear ya', I wish that I could'a been out there thirty years ago with you, and no one else around. It must have been awesome having the whole deep water to yourself for all of those years."

"Canoe, there's two ways to look at changes that occur in your life that you have no control over. You can accept them and try to go with the flow, or you could deny them and struggle both within yourself and outside yourself in hopes that these changes will somehow just disappear. Sometimes they do but more often than not, they don't. Canoe, everyone wants to get into the act these days. Everyone wants to make a livin' out here on the sound. They see what we catch when the run's on in the summertime and the weather's good. And they think "O.K. what a peaceful and free way of life we got out here, and that we're all makin' a million bucks out here livin' in natural bliss. Mark it well Canoe, things are gonna start changin' big time."

Davey kept fishing his own gear, and he helped Vinnie set his in. Then Buddy on the Mister Starbuck needed a hand setting out his gear so Davey helped him out. Buddy was tough as nails. He was in his late fifties, and very wealthy, and owned his own dock just downstream of the state launching ramp, and just south of where Davey kept his dory. He lobstered for a hobby more than a financial endeavor, but he loved to fish and he loved the "Mister Starbuck," and he loved to be out on the sound.

Davey knew how to run the big boats, thanks to Vinnie. He knew that he'd probably never have a big boat of his own, so this was his chance to run them, and feel how they handled the waves and currents of the sound. And when he was at the helm, and the captains were working the stern, it really made him feel that he was an important part of their life.

Then it became his time to help Ralphie. Ralphie had a house on the water in short beach, in the middle of the western curve of Branford harbor. He was a shell fisherman, clams and oysters. He was a retired sailor who spent twenty years in the Merchant Marines. One day he was there at the launching ramp as Davey paddled in. Davey knew him only from seeing him working the shoreline in his heavy, wide green scow. He always dressed the same, and this day was no exception, with his green khaki shorts and white t-shirt. Ralphie was a solitary man, never married, and Davey was quite surprised to see him face to face.

"I wanna' fish for conch, do you think you could help me out?"

Ralphie asked Davey as he stepped out of his canoe and pulled it aground. Davey looked into the old sailor's eyes and replied, "What do you want of me?"

"I want to build some traps and fish for conch and I've seen you out on the sound for many years, and I figured that maybe we could work together for awhile."

Davey kinda' felt sorry for Ralphie, being a reclusive person, and being alone and all, so he agreed to help him out. First Ralphie needed money for the materials. Davey went out with him onto his shell fishing grounds and over went the hand dredge, a bushel of fine table oysters came aboard after a short tow. Ralphie picked up a select oyster off of the culling board, and began to intensely study it as the scow drifted downstream. Ralphie was fascinated by its shape or size or color or whatever, to a point when after a long minute had gone by, and they were coming precariously close to a line of boats tied off to a float at the edge of the channel, Davey had to shake Ralphie's shoulder to snap him out of the apparent trance that he seemed to be in. Ralphie placed his treasure on the console in front of him, and then he refocused his attention in regards to their present situation. Davey was puzzled as to Ralphie's previous action, maybe it was because of the reclusive nature of both the fisherman as well as his catch.

They caught a bunch of oysters, and they caught a bunch of clams. And then they went and bought some wood lathes and frames and made sixty conch traps. Now they needed bait. Davey knew from Vinnie that horseshoe crabs were the best bait for conch, especially egg bearing females. He also knew from experience that these crabs came up onto the beaches along the shores of the sound in the evenings that brought a high tide on either side of the full moon in June. He'd been down to the vast expanse of sandy beaches in West Haven, and down into Milford with Vinnie when the conditions were right and the large prehistoric crabs with the armor-plated hinged shell and long hard spiny tail came up onto the beaches by the thousands, marching methodically up beyond the high tide level and dig themselves into the moist sand to lay their eggs. Just before breaking the water's surface, the males which were riding atop the female's shells would fertilize the eggs. It was very easy pickings.

Davey brought Ralphie down to the beaches in Ralphie's beat up old pickup loaded with a dozen wooden fish boxes and a couple of metal hooks to drag the boxes along the sandy shore. They arrived at water's edge just before the top of the tide and just as the sun was falling below the horizon and the horseshoe crabs were coming on strong. They each filled their boxes within minutes, then pulled them up above the high tide line. Then there were two more boxes full, then two more and two more.

Davey brought down the six remaining empty boxes to the edge of the water and began dragging the full ones back up to the truck. Then something very amusing happened, the Cat pulled into the parking lot along side of Ralphie's pickup. The Cat was another old reclusive fisherman out of Branford, actually the Farm river, and he also did some conch fishing.

Davey was tired and after loading the six heavy boxes onto the back of the truck, he climbed inside the cab and took some fresh water. Looking out along the beach, he noticed that the Cat had gotten out in front of Ralphie and was feverously loading his two fish boxes with crabs, while pulling them ahead and away from Ralphie, who was increasing his speed, a fish box tagging along behind each arm, in the grip of a metal hook.

Then Davey looked to the western horizon and saw a line of low black clouds quickly approaching their location. Just as the rain and wind and lightening hit, Ralphie had caught up to the Cat, and upon releasing his grip on the fishhooks, thrust his body into the Cat's and knocked him backwards, flat into the water. And as the wind blew and the rain came and the lightening illuminated the darkening sky followed by loud earth reverberating roars of thunder, Davey sat in the dry, safe quarters of Ralphie's cab and watched the two stubborn old solitary fishermen knock each other into the water in an attempt to get their boxes filled first. Davey surmised to himself that maybe that's why some people are so reclusive; that maybe they can't look at the whole picture, maybe they can't look all around them like Albie had asked Davey to do many years before. He supposed that maybe if they did, they might realize that one could always find someone to help you out, if you reached out for it, and that there were enough crabs right there on that beach that it would be easy to get a full truckload for everyone.

It seemed to Davey that the scene that was unfolding in front of him was that from an animated cartoon. As the lightning flashed and illuminated the beach for a brief moment at a time, Davey witnessed the struggle between Ralphie and the Cat in its various ridiculous forms. He was amused, however also sad to see two grown men carrying on in such a manner. Perhaps, he thought, maybe they weren't out there trying to kill each other, chest high in the water in the middle of a thunderstorm just over who could fill their boxes first.

Davey maintained this lifestyle for the next seven years. He had his circle of traps and he fished his nets, and he helped out the other fishermen when they needed help. And he came to realize that what Vinnie had said to him when Davey decided not to fish with him on a full time basis was coming true, that there were many things changing in the sound. Vinnie had a knack for seeing into the future of the sound, and again his anticipation proved to be right.

First came the draggers, big offshore steel boats with long heavy stabilizers, that when lowered gave the areas in which they were working the appearance of a flock of giant metal birds slowly swimming along in a wide stretched out line. Those boats ran big bottom trawls typically fifty to seventy feet wide, with five foot steel doors and a heavy chain fixed to the bottom line and short mats of nylon line tied along its length called "chafing gear." They were dragging for lobsters, which at that time there was no restriction as to how many legal sized lobsters could be harvested in this manner. The trap fishermen knew that there was a high mortality rate on young lobsters, and especially soft shelled lobsters in this process. Furthermore, they figured that these heavy, bottom raking nets were wreaking havoc to the natural environment on the bottom of the sound.

Then came the bunker boats. On any given day there could be seen at least three or four of these huge offshore purse seiners from New Jersey out working the sound. These steel hulled boats were huge, perhaps a hundred and twenty feet long, and they fished out there for days at a time, until their holds were full. A school of bunker would be spotted, finning on the surface. Then a huge net would be paid out in a circular manner, surrounding the school. Then it would be hauled aboard by a large metal drum mounted just forward of the stern. Davey thought it to be a shameful thing when Vinnie told him that the "bunker" were being harvested for use in cat food and fertilizer.

That same year, there was a heavy onslaught of "part-timers" and "ten-potters" in addition to the hundreds of extra traps that the full-timers were fishing; the sound was virtually saturated with buoys.

And this new group of fishermen all set out gillnets in an attempt to harvest their own bait. Out on the sandy bottom off of Sunset beach, just around the corner from Second point at the eastern tip of Branford harbor, where Davey and Albie and Brooksie and the Cigar Man once had sole use of their gillnets and gave each other plenty of "fishin' space" between the nets, there were over twenty nets stretched out along the half mile stretch of beach. Davey had to carefully navigate through the maze. His catch from his net went down dramatically. And his lobster catch started to decline as well.

The sound were being over-fished. Davey learned that it wasn't happening just off the shores of Branford, but generally throughout the entire sound. The over-fishing didn't come just from the commercial guys either. Sports-fishermen were also contributing to the decline of just about everything that was edible or marketable that either swam or crawled or lay as quiet as a clam.

After several years of this heavy onslaught, many species of fish as well as shellfish became scarce in number. The vast schools of "bunker," a commodity baitfish used both commercially and recreationally were reduced to a remnant population of small scattered schools. Blackfish and flounder which were a staple catch for countless years also became hard to find. Even the prolific porgy or "scup," which typically migrated into the sound by the millions in the summertime and stayed until late fall were hard to come by.

In ten years of lobstering on the sound, Davey had seen it all. He was out there when one could make a living fishing two-hundred traps inside out of a small boat. He was out there during the conception of the offshore lobster fishery and he and Vinnie were the first fishermen from Connecticut to venture out to the "other side of the pond." He was out there when greed and sheer numbers and mismanagement decimated a healthy, thriving sound. Now he figured that things would never be as they once were.

Then Davey met someone very special in his life, a beautiful Irish brunette with striking hazel eyes named Deborah. Davey fell in love, and married Deborah, and vowed to get a "real job," in order to make a steady paycheck and raise a family. However, there was one more chapter in his commercial fishing career that remained unwritten.

Chapter 9

Captain Dave

Bart and Anthony decided to give lobstering a try out in the ocean waters off of Rhode Island. They bought a brand-new forty-five-foot steel hulled boat which they named the "Voyager." So they were movin' on out of the sound, into the "Big Pond." This guy Gerry out of Stony Creek bought the thirty-four-foot "Janey M" from Bart, along with six-hundred traps, and seemingly the right to fish Bart's grounds. The other fishermen in the area were made aware of this change.

Gerry was a boat broker, and a part-time inshore lobster fisherman. He had no experience in regards to the mid-sound trawl fishery. He needed a good, experienced stern man. The word got around, and one evening Davey got a call from Gerry.

"I heard that you're the best stern man around. Everyone that you've helped out says that you're the man that I need to get me goin'. They say that you know how to run the big boats, how to tell which end of the trawl to pull first, how to coil the trawl lines on the deck so they don't tangle up. They say that you know when to move the gear when the lobsters are gonna' move. Davey, I'll give you sixty bucks a day or ten percent of the catch, whichever is more, I need you to help me out. Davey didn't jump at Gerry's offer right away, although in the back of his mind he really wanted to. He took some time to think about Gerry's lifestyle. He figured that maybe Gerry was kinda like himself. He sold boats for a living, and he dabbled with a little commercial fishing. And in that regard Davey figured that they might have a few things in common. Davey figured that even though Gerry was a salesman, he didn't sell houses or computers or furniture, or any other land bound material object. Davey figured that Gerry either consciously or sub-consciously sold boats because it was something that gave someone the opportunity to be out in their natural environment, and Davey appreciated that concept, and surely could relate to it.

Davey figured that up to this point in his life, he'd been, and been a part of many fishermen's lives, in one way or another. He felt confident, and well rounded, only because of this diverse group of people. From the Codfather and Vinnie, he saw what it took to be a leader, and he accepted the fact that the time that he had spent with those two very unique fishermen, that he was a follower. And he figured that he did well in that position, and that he had learned a lot from those experiences being in that position, only from acceptance and respect for those who were leading him and were willing to hand down their knowledge. The he thought about Albie and Ralphie, whom he figured were in a third group of people. He thought them to be "lone wolves," people who for one reason or another chose to disassociate with their fellow man for the most part and only let a few people inside their partially open shell. Davey never lived his life in that manner. And when he was called upon to associate with someone that did, he made a point of it to try to open that person's shell up just a little bit more. Lastly, Davey thought, there were people that were just plain helpers. And these people seemed to be the most satisfied and content people of all. And that's the feeling that came upon Davey every time that he had helped the other fishermen out. So now he came to a conclusion. With his experience and knowledge, he felt that this would be a fine opportunity to do two of the things in life that he enjoyed doing most, being a leader and a helper.

"Yeah, I know the boat, and I know Bart's grounds. I helped Bart set in two springs ago. Yeah the 'Janey M,' she's a good boat with a load on, a little rolly when you're pullin' gear in a big swell and a stiff wind, because she's so light and she's got that big flared Novi bow. That two-ninety-two Chevy is a little fussy in the cold weather, but once she's runnin' she's pretty reliable. Best feature of that boat is her dry exhaust. She's a little loud, but that four-inch pipe comin' right up through the middle of the dash sure breaks the chill and warms the hands in a cold blow. Yeah, I've fished with all those guys at one point or another."

Davey wanted to let Gerry know that the other lobster men were telling him the truth. "It's a decent offer Gerry, but I just got married last summer, and I'll have to talk it over with my wife, I'll get back to you." Deborah knew how much Davey loved the water, and how much that he loved trap fishing. Her dream was to marry a fisherman on a boat in Nantucket harbor. Well she got her fisherman and she got Nantucket, however she didn't get on the boat in Nantucket harbor, as the Catholic church would only marry them on dry land. So it was "Saint Mary's Our Lady of the Isle." Anyhow, Deborah let Davey go, "just one more year and that's it," was all that she had to say about the matter.

Gerry was working on his gear, which he had moved to a gravel parking lot alongside a small green marsh with a little creek running through it out to the sound, a block away from the Stony Creek town dock. "Don't put that ground line under the funnel, put it in the like this," Davey reached into the open trap and pulled out the coiled rope. "See, you take the coil and flip it over and put it on top of the funnel so you're not fumblin' around for it when you're on the stern in a heavy chop and all you're doin' is strugglin' to stay in the boat let alone get the gear off in a halfway descent manner. You flip the coil over so it pays out from the top not the bottom because if you don't half the time the whole coil will go over all at once, in a big bird's nest and the trap along with it. And you gotta' always watch the rope, and when you're at the helm, always watch two sets of boots, and the rope."

When I started offshore with Vinnie, one day I wasn't payin' too much attention, I guess I was washin' down the deck or something, when next thing I knew, that ground line had a half hitch around my leg, like a tight relentless hangman's noose, and that taut line to the trap in the water sinkin to the bottom pulled me to the deck and against the stern in a split second. Vinnie had seen what had happened and the "Lady" was in neutral but out on the water you can't stop on a dime. Fortunately, I was able to point my foot down quick enough so that the line just pulled my boot off and sucked it down into the wash. Gotta' wear boots, a little loose is best, no laces, never laces.

Davey helped Gerry get the gear ready, going through every trap with meticulous attention in regards to its ability to catch and hold a keeper as Albie and Vinnie had impressed upon him.

All the gear was ready for the water, and they had a neat load of fifteen trawls, forty-five traps on the boat, as they shoved off from the Stony Creek town dock. Davey noticed that the sky was black far to the north; however, at this point he kept that fact to himself. Gerry was beside himself, beaming with pride and anticipation as he headed out through the channel which wound and turned through the myriad of islands that encompass the thimbles and shelter the fishermen who ply these inland waters.

When they achieved the open waters of the sound, Davey realized that the black sheer line of clouds to the north was bearing down on them; however he chose to wait a little longer before he shared that fact with Gerry, who was steaming at a pretty good clip and looking straight ahead. "Gerry, you're goin' out in the deep water now, and it's time that you focus on that. You gotta get your head out of that office and away from that computer and telephone. And you gotta become totally connected with your natural environment. Like most of the people in modern society these days, they're into all of this technology and they don't look all around to see that we're part of the natural, beautiful, ever changing, ever inspiring world in which we live in. When you're runnin' this boat, you always gotta look close, so we don't hit nothin', and you always gotta look far, all around you, in the sky, on the water to see what's in store. Now look back to the west and I think that we should be headin' back for a bit because we're gonna get a hell of a squall real quick."

Gerry looked back and when he saw the dark low line of clouds bearing down on them, his eyes opened wide and he swiftly reversed course and headed back towards the safety of the islands. The wind picked up to gale force in a matter of minutes, and the sky was full of electricity, and the water turned all white, with a high quick chop. However they were only a short distance from the safety of the islands and after a brief, harrowing steam, they were in the lee of the storm.

Gerry became to know and appreciate Davey for what he was all about. He became a part of Davey's unbounded love and respect and connection to the earth in which they lived on. And he had a lot of respect in regards to Davey's experience and knowledge and wisdom in the task at hand.

Gerry however, right in the beginning suffered what could have been a very tragic, possibly even a career ending loss. They had set in four lines of one hundred traps each, and now it was time to pull the "A" line for the first time, their farthest line to the west, halfway between the Branford reef and Townsend's ledge.

At first light, they arrived on the range; however no half white and half lime green buoys were in sight. Gerry steamed south on his bearing but the line of traps were gone! Thirty-three trawls, ninety-nine traps were gone. A boat appeared to the southwest "Vinnie!" Davey exclaimed after studying the vessel with the binoculars. Without saying a word, Gerry pulled a large fillet knife from its sheath on the dash and steamed towards one of Vinnie's white buoys with the black letters.

Davey remembered the day long ago when he was at the helm of the "Lady" and Vinnie was settin' the trawls, dancing between the ropes, smoke bursting in quick white clouds from the ever-present pipe clutched in his jaws. It was a hard southwesterly blow in late April, with a building wide, deep swell, a sea that one didn't wish to be quartering into with five thousand pounds of traps stacked six feet high in the cockpit.

Davey couldn't hold her on the compass bearing of one-sixty-five with any confidence; the "Lady" was rolling too much. So he put her right into the wind, without telling Vinnie that he had changed course, although he figured that Vinnie knew and thought that Davey had done the right thing, as their trip became much more manageable.

The next day, they were picking up the line and moving it back to its proper location, when out of nowhere this white boat steamed right over to them, and this guy jumped on the "Lady," and kicked Vinnie right in the ribs, sending him to the deck in pain. "Get this fuckin' gear outta' my grounds right now, and don't ever let me catch you over here again." The New Haven boys were tough, and they were mean, and they were ruthless.

Gerry grabbed up the buoy, however just as he raised the knife to cut it clean, Davey grabbed hold of his arm. "Vinnie didn't do it, it's your initiation. It's the New Haven boys tryin' to get the Branford boys into a big war with each other. They figure that if we cut each other's lines that there'll be more lobsters gettin' through for them to catch."

Davey could feel the tension easing in Gerry's arm. "Come on, let's get out the grapple, and see if we can't find some of the gear." Gerry bit the bullet, and calmed down, and accepted what Davey had said to be the truth. They grappled up most of the "A" line from its temporary grave on the bottom of the sound, and they tied on new buoy lines and new buoys that Davey had made sure that they had stored in the cabin. And after a long day they had some semblance of an "A" line, and made the long steam home.

After that incident, things calmed down, and Gerry and Davey had a fairly successful summer. Davey showed Gerry how to tighten up the space between the trawls when the shedder run was taking place, and how to follow the shedder run out from shallow water into mid-sound as the deeper water warmed. He showed Gerry how to bait the bags with soft bait, bunker or mackerel on the bottom and hard bait, sea robin or skate, on top, so that the traps would fish longer in the warm summer waters. Davey showed Gerry the tiny clear blotches on the underside of the doors on the wooden traps, and let him know that this was the first sign that it was comin' on worm season. And the female lobsters were now beginning to show up with fresh green eggs tucked under their wide fanned out tails. Worm season, and green egger season, time to haul 'em in and dry 'em out.

Over the summer, Gerry had bought up a couple hundred used wire traps from fishermen up and down the shoreline, as they brought in the wooden traps to dry, Davey and Gerry brought out the wire traps to fish out to the middle of the sound. There always seemed to be a good number of lobsters out there in the middle, even though the real summer or fall run wasn't going on. So they kept at it, right through worm season.

It came to be September, September 12, to be exact, a day and date that Davey and Gerry will most assumedly never forget. A clear dawn sky found them making their way out of the shelter of the thimbles, on their way out to the gear. A fresh westerly breeze had spawned foamy white tops on the high wide lurching swell. They gained the bobbing and clanging red bell which marks brown's reef and eased southward, the boat rolling quite heavily in the quartering sea. Off to the southeast, Davey spotted something unusual. It looked like a big wooden cone bobbing up and down, within sight in the crest of the high swell, then disappearing in the trough.

"Gerry, there's something out there to the southeast, something big driftin' almost underwater," Davey announced, his outstretched arm and finger pointing in the direction of his sighting. Gerry changed course and after a few minutes, both men felt an eerie chill go up their spine upon seeing that this was indeed the bow of a big wooden cabin cruiser struggling to say above the surface in the heavy swell.

Gerry turned to channel sixteen on the V.H.F. radio and alerted the Coast Guard in New Haven harbor, about ten miles away from their present location, as to what they had discovered. Then the two fishermen began a search pattern in the form of ever widening circles, Davey intensely scrutinizing the endless expanse of water with a good pair of binoculars.

After about an hour, the circle had grown to about four miles across, and they were now in its southwest quadrant when Davey spotted something out of place, far off to the southwest. "Gerry, over there," he rasped. "It looks like a big bunch of different colored buoys all tied together." Gerry pushed the "Janey M" hard into the swell.

To their horror, they came upon four bodies lying, clinging seemingly lifeless to an array of buoys and life jackets and bumpers, and anything that would float, tied together in a desperate makeshift raft. Gerry eased upwind and turned the "Janey M" broadside to the mess of plastic and humanity. Davey kicked off his boots and jumped overboard, and grabbed on to the very unstable floating mass. He shielded the four people on the raft from being slammed into by the idling "Janey M" and one by one the two fishermen pulled the seemingly lifeless bodies aboard.

Two girls, middle aged girls, lay pale and unconscious on the deck, but they had pulses, they were both still alive. One thin middle aged man slowly began to move, while lying face down on the deck, as if he was coming out of hibernation. The other man, who was fairly heavyset, slowly rolled to his side and sat up shivering uncontrollably.

Davey climbed down into the cabin and quickly reappeared with everything that he could find that was dry and warm. He and Gerry huddled the four people together on the deck behind the engine box and covered them up as best that they could. Gerry grabbed the mike and notified the Coast Guard that they had found four people: two males and two females, and they were about five miles south of Branford harbor, steaming in that direction. He also let them know that the two females were unconscious, and apparently in the advanced stages of hypothermia, and that one of the men was not much better off and the other was in pretty tough shape.

At the same moment, the heavy set guy sprang up from the huddled group, shivering uncontrollably. He made a staggered dash towards the council and grabbed the steaming hot exhaust pipe that sprang from the dashboard amid ships, and went out to vent above the roof, with his numb hands. The smell of scorched skin immediately filled the crisp midmorning air. Davey grabbed one arm and Gerry grabbed the other and together they ripped the man's hands away from the scorching pipe.

The man just stood there, apparently in shock, staring at his steaming outstretched hands. Davey helped him back under the blankets and extra rain gear with the other slumping bodies. A half an hour later, they made it into Branford harbor. The town dock was lit up like a Christmas tree with flashing lights from rescue boats in the water, and rescue and support vehicles on land. Two ambulances were on land, and a forty-one foot Coast Guard cutter as well as the town police boat were idling in the river.

Within minutes, the two ambulances were racing off to a hospital in New Haven with the four stricken boaters. The captain of the Coast Guard cutter had lots of praises for the two fishermen, and let them know that they had probably saved those four people's lives, and that when they received the call that the four people were on board, they decided to steam to Branford Point instead of trying to make a risky transfer in a heavy swell. The four people fully recovered. However, none of them ever called Gerry or Davey to grant a simple "thanks." A couple weeks later, Davey received a certified document in the mail. The letter was from the Coast Guard commander in chief, Group Long Island Sound. It was a letter of accommodation and it read as follows:

Dear Mr. Lubeski,

I would like to take the time to commend you for the rescue you performed on 12 September, 1985, while aboard the fishing vessel "Janey M." Without your willingness to assist, and with the professionalism with which you performed the rescue, these people would have surely perished. Your actions on that day are in keeping within the highest traditions of the Maritime community.

You will be happy to note that three of the people that you rescued were treated and released from the hospital, and the fourth, Gail Lupoli, is quickly recovering and should be released shortly. Again, my personal "Thanks and well done" to you and Mister Vincent, for your quick actions and your dedication to your fellow man.

Sincerely,
D.H. Lyon
Commander
Group Long Island Sound

There's a fishing boat anchored on the reef just northwest of the Cow and Calf. A thin middle aged man wearing only a pair of cut-off, blue jeans and worn-out top siders covered with layers of fish scales sits back in a swivel chair behind the helm. His legs are crossed and stretched out straight with his feet resting on the wide starboard gunwhale. In his hands is a short, stiff boat rod with an ancient bait casting reel attached to the fore end. It's a splendid mid-fall day, a bright blue sky with a few long high streams of clouds, almost a mackerel sky, Captain Dave thought out loud.

Captain Dave gently lifted the tip of the rod up and down, up and down, feeling the light sinker scrape along the surface of the large mussel bed fifteen feet below the surface. It was almost twenty years from his experience on the "Janey M." Captain Dave was now the proud owner of a beautiful twenty-two foot "Seahawk." She's a heavy glass hull with a fairly hard chine, wide beam, a vee birth cuddy and an extended hard top. The "Dancing Girl," is powered by a one hundred and forty horsepower Evenrude motor, and as Captain Dave looks back, she's a far cry from his first vessel. He'd stuck with lobstering and gill-netting over the years as a "part-timer," bringing out his daughter Kelly, and young son Danny, to let them experience what had been his first love in life for a good number of years. Captain Dave made a little extra money on the side, and kept connected with the local commercial fishing industry until the first big lobster die-off hit the sound in 1996.

It was a tragedy for commercial lobstering in the sound. There was a good run going on in the middle, in late October, when suddenly there were hundreds of lobsters coming up dead in the traps. And many more of the creatures that were still alive would die on the way in, in the live tanks on the boats. After that the inshore lobster fishery became virtually non-existent, and Captain Dave packed it in.

The lobstermen came to the conclusion that the die-off was caused by the chemicals that the state was spraying in the marshes to kill mosquitoes. There had been a small outbreak of West Nile virus in the human population along the coastal waters of the sound along the shores down to the west. The lobstermen knew that the mosquitoes carried the disease and transmitted it to humans. And they also figured that the authorities sprayed the chemicals with no foresight or testing in regards to this actions consequence. And they figured that these chemicals washed out into the sound in a natural manner and had a devastating effect on the fragile ecosystem in the sound. However, the authorities would never admit to such a blunder.

Now Captain Dave just fishes for fish, and makes a point of it to connect with and communicate with, and travel a little along the shoreline to experience with people who just fish for fish. The huge schools of menhaden with large hungry bluefish erupting skyward in their midst were gone. The authorities had made it clear to the public that the mature bluefish were contaminated with P. C. B.'s, which is a manmade substance used in making plastic and electrical transformers. The residue from this process has been dumped into the rivers and estuaries that feed the sound and other mid-Atlantic waters for generations.

At this point, Captain Dave refrains from harvesting the big blues on a regular basis, and restricts his diet of these delicious creatures to only a couple meals a year. He was very upset in regards to the fact that again, by lack of concern or foresight, this once thriving recreational fishery for human consumption became a veritable total loss, or so he thought.

Captain Dave heard that they were catching big blues off of the Tomalson Street bridge in New Haven. He went down there to check it out one early evening with his ancient surf casting rod that he had bought from his long gone friend Joe Ciagilia. The rocks below the bridge on either side of the river were nearly shoulder to shoulder with fishermen. There was a small school of menhaden milling just beyond casting distance which would occasionally become airborne in small pockets as a big blue would charge into the pack.

He didn't fish; he just observed and talked to some of the fishermen. People were catching fish, as a fairly large school of big blues pushed the menhaden up almost to the edge of the rocky shore, Captain Dave talked about the fact that these mature bluefish were probably contaminated with potentially cancer causing chemicals and that one shouldn't eat too many of them in the course of a year. The answer that he heard from lots of them was that they were aware of the danger, however most of them were very poor and they were catchin' fish when they could to feed their families and that's the way that it was and that's the way that it always had been. Great, Captain Dave thought to himself; subsistence fishermen catching polluted fish that they had been no part of in regards to their being contaminated, and probably had no say in regards to why they had been contaminated, or what could possibly be done to reverse the trend. They just continued to catch and eat the contaminated fish and ate them and accepted the fact that they were at a health risk in doing so because this was the way it was and is, part of their survival. And it was the same situation with the striped bass as well. Both of these species migrate into these polluted waters during their traditional spring and fall journey up and down the East Coast. However, the stripers rarely give the subsistence fishermen a chance to put them on the dinner table. That fishery has become a commodity and recreation mainly for people with boats, or the means to travel by land to where they're being caught from shore.

The hundreds of buoys that had marked the hundreds of lobster traps that had covered every reef and submerged rocky places along the shoreline were a thing of the past. And the dark green and orange and black native lobsters were gone. And the reliable heavy run of fall blackfish had dwindled to an isolated, scattered bunch of small schools that moved about the reefs. An almost indiscernible tug at the end of the line woke Captain Dave from his daydream. He lowered the rod tip down to the water's surface and when the line became taut once more he pulled back, setting the hook in a quick deliberate manner.

The four pound blackfish gave him a good battle, repeatedly bulldozing down head first in an attempt to gain the security of a rocky crevice; however, Captain Dave refused to let that happen and soon had the fish flapping on the deck of the "Dancing Girl." The blackfish had come up on the hump, in the middle of the outgoing tide to feed on the heavy set of small blue mussels. Captain Dave had four nice fish in the boat in a matter of fifteen minutes; that's currently the limit. A handful of other fishing boats were anchored up tight to the two rocks that showed above the surface. Not one fisherman in any of those boats had even gotten a bite. Captain Dave knew that the bottom around those two rocks was hard sand, not very likely to attract any reef-going blackfish.

Captain Dave put the fishing rod back in the cabin and resumed his position in the swivel chair, legs crossed, feet up on the wide gunwale. He sat back for a long while and listened to the seagulls cry. There was a grey yearling in the group crying like a baby. And he felt the northwest breeze freshening on his face. And he saw those big puffy white balloons coming towards him just above the horizon in the otherwise bright-blue cloudless sky. He got up and started the "Dancing Girl." As the motor warmed up with a steady purr, he climbed around the side of the cabin and up onto the bow. He unfastened the anchor line and methodically drew the vessel over the anchor. Then with a sharp jerk on the line, freed it from its position in the cluster of mussels below. As the boat drifted back in the current, he made his way back around the side of the cabin, anchor rope coiled in hand. As he leaned over the rail to pull up the remaining anchor line and chain, he heard some people talking in the other boats.

"Who is that guy? How come he caught fish and no one else even had a bite?" Then someone on another boat replied, "That's

Captain Dave, he knows the water." And with that, Captain Dave put the boat in gear and as he came about, gave the other fishermen a nod and a wave. Then he pointed the bow toward the distant harbor and began steaming home.

And on the way, he thought to himself, yeah, Captain Dave, how many voyages? A thousand times out and back. He thought again for a time and he said to himself, no more like two. Then he looked back at the boats clustered around the two rocks that protruded above the surface of the sound. They were growing larger with the outgoing tide yet growing smaller and smaller as the distance grew between him and them.

Captain Dave turned his attention back to the bow and continued to close in on the shoreline and at that point in his journey, he gave thanks to the higher power above. He gave thanks for the beautiful trip. And he gave thanks for the beautiful catch. And he gave thanks for every trip that had preceded the current one. This was Captain Dave's routine as he entered the beckoning safety of the two long, high granite arms of the harbor. As he approached the town dock, Captain Dave thought back to a time long ago.

It was early fall, and local natives were gathered, sharing home cooked native seafood, as well as their harvest from their gardens. And talking of times old and new, he remembers when Albie would be there and Brooksie, Whitey, Snowshoe, and the Cigar Man, now all long gone, would be there at this special time to share their lives' bounty and harvest with the others. He remembers the Cigar Man talking about how in early winter they would go up to the gravely bend in the river, just below Dutch Wharf boat yard, and scoop up silver hake with large long handled homemade nets. Brooksie and Albie reminisced out lout to an attentive audience about how they used to row out to the beacon and come back with a bushel of blackfish to share with their family and neighbors. He sees Whitey's stone faced profile in the flickering light of a kerosene lantern behind the legion, bluefish pole in hand, staring out onto the water in the darkening sky. He remembers the large meaty weather beaten hand of Snowshoe as it deposits a morning's worth of wriggling shiners into Davey's empty pail. He hears the voice of his long gone friend Joe Ciaglia speaking of the times in the fall when one could fish off of the town dock and catch enough blackback flounder, as he deftly rolled a guide on a custom rod.

Those days are gone now, Captain Dave thought to himself. The bluefish and stripers are coming back, but you're not supposed to eat too many of them, due to pollution. The old timers were lucky not to have seen those days. And Captain Dave felt lucky to have spent a good deal of his life working and fishing with them and sharing his energy and youth and listening to their tales.

The whiting are gone now, and the flounder and mackerel and tommy cod too. And the lobsters are a mere remnant population. The old timers had their memories and they shared them, some more freely than others. Upon passing the dock, Captain Dave gave one last look back. He saw a young boy fishing alone with his bike parked next to him, and Davey said to himself out loud, "time to go snapper fishing."